NATHAN MACKINNON
The NHL's Rising Star

Paul Hollingsworth

NIMBUS
PUBLISHING LTD
nimbus.ca

It is because of tragedy that we give such importance to our games.
—Unknown

Nimbus Publishing Limited
3731 Mackintosh St, Halifax, NS B3K 5A5
(902) 455-4286 nimbus.ca

Printed and bound in Canada

NB1199

Cover photo: The Canadian Press Images / Larry MacDougal
Photos on pages 2-5, 7, and 14 courtesy of the MacKinnon family.
Design: Jenn Embree

Library and Archives Canada Cataloguing in Publication

Hollingsworth, Paul, 1969-, author
Nathan MacKinnon : the NHL's rising star / Paul Hollingsworth.
Issued in print and electronic formats.
ISBN 978-1-77108-331-7 (paperback).—ISBN 978-1-77108-332-4 (pdf)

1. MacKinnon, Nathan, 1995-. 2. Hockey players—Canada—Biography. 3. Cole Harbour (N.S.)—Biography. I. Title.

GV848.5.M24H65 2015   796.962092   C2015-904335-2
                                           C2015-904336-0

Canada

Canada Council   Conseil des arts
for the Arts   du Canada

Nimbus Publishing acknowledges the financial support for its publishing activities from the Government of Canada through the Canada Book Fund (CBF) and the Canada Council for the Arts, and from the Province of Nova Scotia. We are pleased to work in partnership with the Province of Nova Scotia to develop and promote our creative industries for the benefit of all Nova Scotians.

TABLE OF CONTENTS

FOREWORD

I was fortunate enough to do play-by-play on television for many of Nathan MacKinnon's games with the Halifax Mooseheads during his brief yet spectacular career in the Quebec Major Junior Hockey League (QMJHL). It was fascinating not only to watch him play, but also to see how he dealt with the expectations of being a hometown superstar, which isn't always easy. A few things stick out for me:

▶ **Witnessing his first playoff goal as a Moosehead.** With his team on the power play, MacKinnon rolled off a Moncton defender at the left-wing boards, deked another defenceman to the ice, and faked out the goalie before stuffing the puck in the net. To me, that play showed what MacKinnon was all about: tremendous leg drive, remarkable stickhandling skills, a terrific finishing touch, and, perhaps above all, irrepressible hunger. I still watch that goal on YouTube every so often.

▶ **Taking in a Mooseheads morning skate during the 2013 QMJHL playoffs in Rouyn-Noranda.** The team was doing line rushes and in that mostly quiet setting, the dominant sound was MacKinnon's skates chewing up the ice when his line took its turn. From the start of his QMJHL career, it was easy to see what a fast and powerful a skater MacKinnon was, but that morning I could actually hear it.

▶ **How he took over the Memorial Cup, leading Halifax to the CHL title.** There were a lot of terrific prospects at that tournament, and some question as to who would be picked first in the impending 2013 NHL Draft. After recording two hat tricks and outshining everyone else as MVP, the question had been answered. Once again, MacKinnon had dominated on the biggest stage, something he's made a habit of during his burgeoning career.

In this informative and entertaining book you are about to read, Paul Hollingsworth mentions feeling a tie to MacKinnon in part because they are both Nova Scotians. I know what Paul means, and if you're a "Bluenoser," I'm guessing you feel the same. We're people of a small province, and we feel a sense of pride when one of "us" succeeds the way MacKinnon has. Nathan comes from a good family. He carries himself the right way. He takes the time to be polite and speak to the fans that approach him. In short, it's easy to root for Nathan MacKinnon. It doesn't hurt that he is an electrifying hockey player whose skill and determination should make him an NHL superstar for years to come.

I'll conclude with a personal story: In September 2014, I received some interest from TSN Radio 690 in Montreal to possibly become the new English voice for the Canadiens. My audition was to call a game at the Bell Centre between the Habs and the Colorado Avalanche. I wasn't necessarily nervous leading up to the game, but for some reason it was a comfort to know MacKinnon would be playing that night. It turns out he was the best player on the ice… nothing new for him. I have to say, I felt a bit of pride every time he touched the puck.

Like so many others, I look forward to watching Nathan's career continue to develop. He's worked extremely hard every step of the way and he deserves nothing but the best.

—**Dan Robertson**
Play-by-play voice of the Montreal Canadiens on TSN Radio 690
August 2015

INTRODUCTION

Life is not always easy. To balance the wonderful highs we also must endure some lousy lows. I've been blessed with incredible friends and family, but in my earlier years I was never the athlete I wanted to be, nor was I the academic achiever my parents thought I could be. I take comfort in knowing that I have enjoyed some modest success in my career and I have a home life that brings me swells of pride, though success has never come easily to me.

I've figured out that life is hard, but I've actually come to embrace the inexact science of living and now look forward to tackling difficult challenges as they arise.

As they say, "It is because of tragedy that we give such importance to our games."

Thank goodness for sports, athletes, fans, and games in general. They make up a significant portion of the fabric of my life. I've seen parts of the world and covered sports events that I never I imagined I would or could. It's what makes me happy and I attach tremendous importance to our games.

The book you are about to read is complete and I'm proud of that accomplishment. Although I wrote the book, this is not my story. It's Nathan's.

Nathan MacKinnon and I have very little in common, except for two things. First, we both come from the same place: Nova Scotia. It's a tie that binds us. To me, sharing these cultural and geographic roots is central. He's my people, and maybe as he grows he will see people like me as his people as well. Maybe he already does.

The second thing we have in common: hockey. Admittedly he's a world-class hockey player and I was (at best) a mediocre university intramural player, but he loves it and I love it too. In this country, sharing a passion for hockey is a big part of our overall Canadian experience. Every player, every fan, and every journalist are linked by one lofty truth: when it comes to hockey in Canada, we are all in this together.

I don't cheer for the Colorado Avalanche—the team I like the most is Montreal, but in my role with TSN I try to turn the fan switch to "off" when I'm covering the NHL—but I do cheer for MacKinnon. He's worked hard his entire life to hone his skills. He was born to play. What's not to like?

This is a young man who took a gamble and left home in junior high to live in Minnesota and play prep school hockey—all in the name of pursuing a high level of development for his special talents. The gamble paid off, and he became a superstar within five years. But in getting there he made a profound sacrifice: he essentially trimmed two years off of his childhood by leaving home at such a young age.

This also a young man who, when told he wasn't "good enough" or "ready" to try out for Canada's national junior team at sixteen, kept his mouth shut, didn't complain, and didn't say anything negative. But he did react. The reaction came on the ice when, the very next day, he scored five goals for the Halifax Mooseheads in a QMJHL regular season game. He'd been denied a place among junior hockey's elite and the very next day he went out and had one of the best nights ever for a single player in the history of Canadian major junior hockey.

This is the same young man who struggled when he finally did play for Canada at the World Junior Hockey Championship and when he returned to the regular season with the Mooseheads, he sprained his knee and missed six weeks of action. But when he stepped back onto the ice, he played some of the best hockey of his career, helping his team secure the 2013 Memorial Cup Championship.

WHAT'S NOT TO LIKE?

What I admire most is Nathan's commitment to excellence. The notion that players like MacKinnon are born predestined for NHL greatness is fool's gold. He clearly has talent but that amounts to, in my opinion, just a portion of what it takes to achieve hockey excellence.

(facing page) Nathan MacKinnon takes a shot on goal against the Phoenix Coyotes during the first period of a game on February 28, 2014, in Denver.
ASSOCIATED PRESS / JACK DEMPSEY

For years Nathan MacKinnon was the best minor hockey player in Nova Scotia. Then he was the best player at Shattuck-St. Mary's High School in Minnesota. He followed that up by being the top-ranked teenaged hockey prospect in the world. I could go on, but suffice to say he's been excellent at every turn of his young career.

And—at every turn he's been compared to Sidney Crosby. It's easy to see how this has happened: they come from the same province, the same neighbourhood (relatively speaking), the same minor hockey roots, the same prep school, and they both had similar junior hockey and NHL draft experiences. They've walked the same paths at many of the same junctures in their hockey lives. Canada Winter Games Head Coach Chris Donnelly has said these comparisons "were probably unfair to Nathan" and he is right. But the comparisons are understandable. I admit, I've been guilty of making them myself.

"I knew right off the hop that I was never going to be Sidney," MacKinnon once told the *Toronto Sun*. "I admire his game but, other than that, I know I'm not him. The comparisons are made because of where I'm from, but I'm just trying to create my own game and be known for what I do myself."

But MacKinnon has risen above it all, never allowing these comparisons to slow him down or hold him back. Over the years he's carved out his own niche, written his own story, and blazed his own on-ice trails.

Clearly, to all who watch him, he's a different player than Crosby; he's bigger, bulkier, and, though he may not put up the point totals that Crosby has over the years, MacKinnon has proven he's worthy of his Crosby-esque stature. He's just entering his twenties and already he's established his own personal hockey brand: he's not physically built like Crosby and his style of play, while similar to Crosby's, is more of a traditional power forward. He's worked hard to prove to himself and others that he's *not* just another version of Sidney Crosby. He's Nathan MacKinnon: a young star who has shown that the best of what he can do is yet to come.

He's made sacrifices, endured adversity, left home at a young age, and has faced pressures that could be too much for men and women twice his age and he's handled it well at every turn. Nathan MacKinnon was displaying professional qualities long before he became a professional athlete. Good for him. It's why I like him and it's why I like to watch him play. These are all sterling qualities—and they help explain why he's grown to enjoy such a huge level of popularity at such a young age.

WHY I WROTE THIS BOOK

I've written this book to appeal to young people. Sure it's for grownups too, but I wanted young hockey fans to be the primary audience. I love hanging at the rink and watching my children and their teammates play. If those readers enjoy this book, I will deem it a success.

Something I continually strive for is "cultivating a discipline of gratitude." For me, these are words to live by. I'm especially grateful that a guy like me who grew up with parents who could never afford to own their own home or buy a new car has been able to craft his own life story. There were times when money, or lack thereof, formed a dark cloud over our home. It taught me resilience. How could I not be grateful for that? I think I learned it from my wife, my parents, my teachers, and, through learning a bit about my family history, my grandparents.

I know there are many young people living in my community who need assistance, and they remind me of myself growing up. If a little boy or girl's parents in Dartmouth can't afford skates or hockey registration, that resonates with me. I have decided to donate royalties from this book to the Dartmouth Whalers Minor Hockey Association to allow children who can't afford to play hockey, the game that has become prohibitively expensive. These are my people and having the opportunity to help is something I take seriously.

Some of these kids may wind up as my children's teammates at the Bowles Arena or the Dartmouth Sportsplex. And one, maybe even two, might wind up being MacKinnon or Crosby-esque with their abilities, worthy of having someone publish their story.

In writing this book I have relied on my own interviews with Nathan MacKinnon, his mother, Kathy, his friends, and former coaches. But in order to cast as broad a net as possible, I also relied on the treasure trove of materials that exist on Nathan and his career thus far. The *Chronicle-Herald*, *Metro News*, The Associated Press, ESPN.com, TSN.ca, and *The Denver Post* have all covered MacKinnon's career splendidly. Their work has been invaluable to help fill in a few blanks in my overall narrative. I applaud their fine work.

I thank you advance for your support. Enjoy the book!

1 THE EARLY YEARS

Nathan MacKinnon's hockey story did not begin in a rink, but on a lake. It's a familiar storyline known to many who have grown up playing the game in Canada.

"Nathan initially took to skating very quickly. Skating was his thing," said his mother, Kathy, in an interview at her home during her son's second NHL season. "We had a lake in our backyard so when arenas were not available, Graham [Nathan's father] would spend time flooding a makeshift ice surface so Nathan could play."

It didn't take long for Nathan's parents to notice their son's special talent for the game. Perhaps they didn't foresee a National Hockey League career, but it was obvious that he was one of the better child hockey players in Nova Scotia.

"Clearly we noticed when playing in minor hockey that skating was a strong skill," said Kathy. Nathan would dominate every level of minor hockey he played in—novice, atom, peewee, and bantam.

"I first met Nathan as a first year peewee player in Cole Harbour when he was eleven years old," said former minor hockey head coach Jon Greenwood. "My brother and I were coaching the peewee AAA team. We were well aware of him after he scored 135 goals in atom the year before. He was a dynamic little player. Not just fast, but amazingly quick laterally. And he loved to play. Was hungry and never got bored."

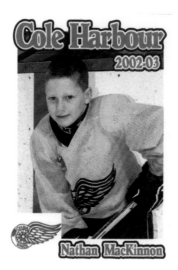

Nathan MacKinnon
#19

TIMBITS 2
Purple Lightning

Position: Forward
Birth Place: Halifax, NS
Birth date: September 01, 1995

Nathan loves watching those Moosehead games! Local hockey fans say that he plays like a young Eric Lindros! The Philadelphia Flyers hope to sign him to a multi-million dollar contactin 2015! The Mooseheads would love to get Nathan's Quebec major-junior playing rights!

CHBA
2000/01

Nathan MacKinnon
 # 19

Cole Harbour
Novice Stingers

Position: Center
Birth Place: Halifax, NS
Birth Date: September 1, 1995

Nathan has a powerful slapshot and many fans compare him to a young Joe Sakic! Goaltenders simply don't have time to get set when this guy gets the puck. The Mooseheads are bidding for his playing rights. Colorado scouts are closely watching Nathan's games!

CHBA HOCKEY
2002/2003

Nathan MacKinnon
 # 9

Cole Harbour Wings
Novice Tier 1

Position: Forward/Center
Birth Place: Halifax, NS
Birth Date: September 1, 1995

Nathan has a powerful slapshot like Alex Tanguay and can score from anywhere! He always works hard and has impressed Colorado scouts with his impassioned effort on every shift! Nathan is billet brother to Halifax Mooseheads Freddy Cabana and Maxime Trotter!

CHBA HOCKEY
2003/2004

Nathan's Timbits and novice hockey cards (L-R): age five, seven, eight.

Greenwood coached MacKinnon in his first year of peewee hockey, and again in bantam when he was thirteen. He took notice of MacKinnon's competitiveness at a very young age. "Nathan always loved the game and his competitiveness was off the charts," said Greenwood. "He never wanted to come off the ice. He never wanted a practice or a shift to end.

"One of my favourite memories is just how he would challenge me as a coach to any type of competition: accuracy, shooting, or one-on-one drills. Here's this kid who is eleven, twelve years old and he's challenging me, an adult in his mid-twenties. He would have a completely straight face and expected to beat you—he would be crushed if he didn't. The funny part is, even at that age, he would win more than he would lose."

As a twelve-year-old (peewee-aged) player, playing bantam AAA for the Cole Harbour Red Wings and competing against children one and two years older than him, MacKinnon dominated: he had 110 points in just 50 games and led his team to the Atlantic championship. He followed that up the next season with 145 points in just 35 games—an average of more than 4 points per game.

It was a performance that garnered attention across the province. Like Sidney Crosby before him, Nathan MacKinnon's fame as a bantam hockey super-achiever began to grow. At only thirteen years old, he was a hockey prodigy and was already receiving attention from media and fans.

"It seemed to be more about being recognized regularly," said his mother, Kathy. "He always handles it so well, taking the time to get pictures with people or signing items. It's always very surreal when we are with him and he is recognized—something you will never get used to."

At home, to the amazement of his parents, Nathan displayed laser beam focus. He wasn't just very good, he was also very determined: "Nathan decided at a very young age, probably around seven years old, that the NHL was his goal," said Kathy. "As he progressed and entered high school, Graham and I would, of course, emphasize the importance of school. We asked the

Nathan (L) and his childhood friend Cole Murphy in 2003, age eight.

question one day, 'If Plan A didn't work out, what would be his Plan B?' His answer was, 'Plan B is just a distraction for Plan A; I will focus on Plan A.' Over the years, Graham would discuss distractions and how to avoid them, so this answer made perfect sense to him."

During his time with the Cole Harbour bantam AAA Red Wings, MacKinnon left the public school system to enroll at the Maritime Hockey Academy (MHA). Back in those early days, it was a private school that combined hockey with academics. Today, it's been renamed the Maritime Varsity Academy—a school with a broader scope when it comes to combining sports and classroom studies. By enrolling at the MHA, Nathan was also putting himself under the tutelage of Jon Greenwood, his bantam AAA head coach, who was the lead instructor at the school.

Nathan (middle) and his Cole Harbour Red Wings team-mates after winning the 2008 provincial championship.

"The Maritime Hockey Academy was a perfect fit for Nathan," said Kathy. "Hockey has always been who he was and embedded into his DNA. It made sense that academics and extra ice time go hand in hand. It was a place where like-minded students attended and teachers had respect for the students that truly loved the game. Jon Greenwood was a mentor to Nathan both on and off the ice. Not only was Jon his teacher in the classroom, he was also coaching him as well. MHA was a place where students could have their dreams and teachers worked with the students to achieve those dreams."

MacKinnon enrolled at the MHA at a time when the school was a fledgling idea: it had students, teachers, instructors, and on-ice programming but because it was so new, no one, not even the people running the school, knew if it would succeed. MacKinnon's enrolment gave it a critical shot in the arm at just the right time. "Nathan gave us instant credibility," said Greenwood. "Having the top twelve-year-old in the Maritimes enroll in our school was, in hindsight, a critical breakthrough."

BANTAM AAA STATISTICS

Year	Team	Games Played	Points
2007–08	Cole Harbour Red Wings	50	110
2008–09	Cole Harbour Red Wings	35	145

Nathan, age eight, as captain of the Junior Mooseheads.

2 SHATTUCK-ST. MARY'S

After two years of dominating bantam AAA in Nova Scotia, it was time for MacKinnon to take his development to a new level and a new locale. In the fall of 2009, following the example of Sidney Crosby, MacKinnon enrolled at Shattuck-St. Mary's: a prestigious private school in Faribault, Minnesota. Just as it had been for Crosby, Nathan's experience was a smashing success.

In his first year, Nathan scored 54 goals and accumulated 101 points in 58 games, but one issue that popped up was his competitive and demanding nature, both of himself and his teammates. "Nathan demanded nothing but the best from himself," Shattuck-St. Mary's coach John LaFontaine told *Metro News*. "He was tough on his teammates; if they weren't ready to play or ready to battle he would really let them know.

"We had to get him to trust in his teammates, that he's going to get the puck back. Once he did that he had 'special' written all over him because it doesn't matter what tools you have, if you can't see the ice, that will stop you. Most of the time Nathan was mad at himself and not at his teammates. I don't think Nathan realized just how much of an effect he had on them until midway through the season."

That year, Shattuck-St. Mary's lost in the championship game at the high school hockey nationals. MacKinnon was a rookie, playing far away from home, but in addition to starring on the ice, he showcased admirable leadership qualities off

(L-R) Nathan's mother, Kathy; his sister, Sarah; Nathan; and his father, Graham, at a Shattuck-St. Mary's game in Minnesota.

the ice. "It was heartbreaking for Nathan," said LaFontaine in his interview with *Metro News*. "But he was the first one putting his arms around his teammates; he was the first one sharing his emotions with them. That stays with me."

It wasn't easy for the MacKinnon family to have their teenage son going to school and playing hockey so far away from home. But for Kathy, the time spent her son spent at the Maritime Hockey Academy was the perfect primer; Nathan was now facing pressure, both on- and off-ice, that would be daunting for hockey players twice his age.

"MHA was a great intro to Shattuck, where academics and hockey were one in the same," Kathy said. "Nathan left [Nova Scotia] in grade nine to attend Shattuck and I would be lying to you if I didn't say that we missed him incredibly. If you ever were doubtful of your decision, you were reinforced when you drove on the grounds of Shattuck. It is a beautiful environment with caring, thoughtful, nurturing people. We knew he was happy there. He made lifelong friends and he truly developed not only as a hockey player, but as a person. I'm sure if you asked Nathan, there were times he found it difficult, but he wouldn't trade anything for that experience. We visited regularly and he had many breaks to come home, so it broke up the distance."

YEAR TWO AT SHATTUCK ST.-MARY'S

In his second year at Shattuck-St. Mary's, MacKinnon followed up his freshman performance by dominating the midget high school hockey AAA division with 45 goals and 93 points in 45 games. In many ways his two years at Shattuck-St. Mary's mirrored Sidney Crosby's time there. Both were enormously successful from an individual and team point of view, and, just like Crosby, MacKinnon followed up his rookie year with an even more successful second season.

While MacKinnon continued his on-ice development and dominance, his team finished the season with heartbreak. Shattuck-St. Mary's made it to the under-16 national championship final, but ultimately lost to the Detroit HoneyBaked, 3–2. Just like when Crosby attended the school, MacKinnon helped lead the Shattuck-St. Mary's team to a high level of national success. He went to Minnesota with two goals: play hockey at higher level, and further propel his overall development. He achieved both in his two years at the prep school.

"It was a privilege to coach Nathan," LaFontaine told *Metro News*. "I just opened the door and let him go. It's so fun to be around players like him, those players you have to pull off the ice they're so hungry."

Shattuck-St. Mary's was also more intense academically than anything MacKinnon had experienced at the Maritime Hockey Academy or would later experience at Prince Andrew High School in Dartmouth. "High school in Minnesota was different from high school at Prince Andrew," said his mom, Kathy. "Shattuck academics came first, and if you didn't have something complete, then hockey would have to wait. Staff lived at school so the right hand always knew what the left hand was doing. They were very strict with the athletes, and it was a great atmosphere to have success in school."

"He could be a perfectionist as a younger student," said Jon Greenwood, who had taught MacKinnon for two years at the Maritime Hockey Academy. "[He was] always asking if something was right or good enough. He didn't want to be wrong or make mistakes."

SHATTUCK-ST. MARY'S BANTAM AND MIDGET AAA STATISTICS

Year	Team	Level	Games Played	Points
2009–10	Shattuck-St. Mary's	Bantam AAA	58	101
2010–11	Shattuck-St. Mary's	Midget AAA	40	93

In December 2010, while still attending Shattuck-St. Mary's, MacKinnon returned to Canada to play for Team Atlantic at the 2011 World U-17 Hockey Challenge in Winnipeg and Portage la Prairie, Manitoba. He was only fifteen and playing as an underage player, but he took the tournament by storm: he scored 5 goals and added 3 assists for 8 points in 5 games.

It was this performance that made Jon Greenwood think that his young protégé might have a long-term, star-studded future in the game of hockey. "There's no question to me that year was his breakout," said Greenwood. "He was, without a doubt, Team Atlantic's best player and the best on the ice in some games. And these were rosters filled with kids already playing major junior."

2011 CANADA WINTER GAMES – HALIFAX, NOVA SCOTIA

Once he was back at school in January, MacKinnon was called upon to suit up and wear his home colours. He returned to Nova Scotia for two weeks in February 2011 to play for Team Nova Scotia at the Canada Winter Games, hosted that year in Halifax.

Since leaving to play for Shattuck-St. Mary's, MacKinnon had become an international hockey celebrity. Dubbed "the next Sidney Crosby" by many, MacKinnon was returning home to play in front of family, hometown fans, and friends for the first time in two years. Plus, he was suiting up for his province.

"I'd had him in camps and had been with him and seen him play along the way," said Team Nova Scotia's head coach Chris Donnelly. "I knew his individual skills were exceptional. To me that skill level was evident, but I wanted to see how he had developed in other areas, how he would interact with his teammates. In these areas he would prove to be exceptional."

"The Canada Games was a great experience [for Nathan]," Kathy MacKinnon said. "He had the opportunity to reunite with so many of the boys he had played spring hockey with and represent his province. Being in Halifax really was a special experience as well, as the hometown crowd was behind the team."

It was at the Canada Games, when Nathan played against his own age group, that Jon Greenwood noticed just how dominant MacKinnon really was: "To me, that's when I thought he could potentially be the best 1995-born player in Canada and possibly beyond. He was outstanding in that tournament."

Crowds at the Halifax Metro Centre and Dartmouth Sportsplex were huge—thousands came out to watch MacKinnon play for his home province. After losing their opening game to Ontario 5–0,

Team Ontario's Alex Yuill (R) checks Team Nova Scotia's Nathan MacKinnon during the 2011 Canada Winter Games in Halifax. THE CANADIAN PRESS / MIKE DEMBECK

MacKinnon and Team Nova Scotia lost their second game to British Columbia 8–3. MacKinnon scored his first goal of the tournament but his team was clearly being outmatched, having been outscored 13–3 through two games.

In their third game, Nova Scotia bounced back with a well-played but tough luck 5–4 shootout loss to Québec—a game they had led 3–1 with six minutes to go in the third period.

Overall in the opening round, MacKinnon scored twice for his team, tallying a total of 3 goals in 3 games. Unfortunately, with a 0–3 record, Nova Scotia sat dead last

in the Pool A standings with a slim chance at advancing to the playoff rounds at the Canada Games.

Still, even in defeat, MacKinnon found ways to distinguish himself. "We were playing that game against Québec and Nathan made a huge effort to block a shot," said head coach Chris Donnelly. "It was really something to have our best player leading in that way. It was very inspiring to the team."

In the qualification round, MacKinnon led Team Nova Scotia by scoring 3 goals and adding 1 assist for a 7–2 win over Newfoundland and Labrador. The next game, Nova Scotia lost another heartbreaker, this time 5–3 to Ontario in the quarter-final, thus ending any shot at winning a medal at the games. They would split their final regulation games, losing 4–1 to Manitoba while beating New Brunswick 5–3.

Overall, Nova Scotia won just twice in seven games but MacKinnon was clearly the dynamic player everyone expected. He scored 8 goals and had 3 assists in 7 games while playing in front of his hometown fans.

"It was tough for him and that team to play at home in that tournament," said Donnelly, "but those kids played well and handled the pressure well. We came very close to beating some very good teams on a pretty big stage. Heading into the Canada Games he was always being compared to Sidney Crosby and I thought that was unfair. But at the games he became associated with the 'Big Three:' along with Québec's

Former Calgary Flames general manager and TSN colour commentator Craig Button on the 2011 Canada Winter Games:

Nathan was the prodigy of the tourney being that he was from neighbouring Cole Harbour and he was following in the footsteps of another prodigy from the same hometown. I had seen Nathan at the under-17 tourney just a few weeks prior, so I had a good idea how talented he was. He was fifteen playing versus sixteen-year-olds and was a very confident player who more than held his own. Anthony Duclair was also there as a fifteen-year-old with Québec so I had familiarity with him also. Curtis Lazar was another top player and very quickly showed his talents. The first game we televised was BC versus Québec and it was a fantastic game with many players who showed enormous potential, Drouin included.

That being said, Nathan was the star attraction and was a catalyst for a Nova Scotia team that had a tremendous following during the games, and nearly qualified for the medal round, falling short in a 5–3 loss to Ontario that featured, among others, Max Domi, Darnell Nurse, and Bo Horvat. MacKinnon was phenomenal and he alone struck fear into the opposition. He was fast and dynamic but what stood out for me was his burning competitiveness. He was always looking to make a difference and would not allow himself to get pushed out of the game. Keep in mind that this was a mismatch of teams only made competitive because of the brilliance of MacKinnon. The crowd was excited watching Nova Scotia play throughout the tourney but it was a game such as this, that I think the realization hit home that Cole Harbour had produced yet another star player.

Jonathan Drouin and BC's Curtis Lazar, he was a top three standout star [of the tournament]."

Back in Minnesota, the Shattuck-St. Mary's team played without Nathan during the Canada Games. The nature of the Games was completely foreign to most of his teammates and coaches. "He had come home from Shattuck-St. Mary's for the Games and it was really interesting that his teammates in Minnesota had never heard of such an event," said Kathy MacKinnon. "It allowed him the chance to gloat about Canada again!"

THE 3 MOOSEHEADS

On June 4, 2011, Nathan MacKinnon was selected first over-all in the Quebec Major Junior Hockey League draft by the Baie-Comeau Drakkar and right away there were doubts that he would report for training camp later that summer.

Baie-Comeau chief scout Pierre Desjardins holds the jersey of the team's first overall pick at the 2011 QMJHL draft.

THE CANADIAN PRESS / JACQUES BOISSINOT

MacKinnon and his family never publicly discussed the reasons, but the young forward and his family saw the Drakkar as a bad fit. Whether it was the city's remote location or concerns about the team itself was unclear; MacKinnon simply did not want to go to Baie-Comeau.

Within days it was reported that MacKinnon had asked for a trade and, failing that, would play in the National Collegiate Athletic Association (NCAA) in the United States. Hockey Canada and NCAA rules dictate that a player must choose one or the other. MacKinnon had leverage when it came to pressing his case and getting his wish: Baie-Comeau could keep him as a drafted player and watch him choose the NCAA, or they could trade him and get a chance to choose a new player from the stockpile. The Drakkar chose to trade him.

Throughout it all, the Halifax Mooseheads were closely monitoring the situation, making sure they were positioned to take advantage should Baie-Comeau make the trade.

"There were a number of teams who wanted Nathan," Mooseheads general manager Cam Russell said. "I think all of the Maritime teams were trying to get him. When Baie-Comeau won the right to pick number one, I let their GM Steve Ahern know we wanted the pick. I really wanted to make sure they knew that no matter what happened going forward, that we were the team that wanted to get that pick from them. They tried to convince Nathan to go to Baie-Comeau. The Drakkar met with Nathan and his family to get them to change their minds. After the selection was made at the draft and they picked Nathan, all we could do was stay close to the situation by always letting Ahern know that we wanted the pick before the draft and we wanted the player."

Within five weeks, MacKinnon got his wish and was traded to his hometown team, the Halifax Mooseheads, in exchange for Carl Gelinas, Francis Turbide, and three first-round picks. MacKinnon would join Halifax and be paired with the number two overall draft pick, Jonathan Drouin.

"When the trade was made I was golfing in the Danny Gallivan tournament, working on the phone all day talking with

Kathy MacKinnon's reflections on her son's two years with the Mooseheads:

We never ever took those days with the Mooseheads for granted. We knew very few players were fortunate enough to play their major junior years at home and we loved every minute of it. Nathan, of course, grew up a huge fan of the Mooseheads and we also billeted Moosehead players for three years. To become a Moosehead himself was very surreal. The excitement of watching your son in a crowded Metro Centre or seeing that jersey on his back would make the hair on our necks stand up. The Mooseheads organization is also first-class, starting with Bobby Smith and Cam Russell. No wonder they have experienced success with this franchise.

Baie-Comeau and [Mooseheads owner] Bobby Smith," said Russell. "It was such a long and drawn-out process. One minute you think you're close, then it falls through, and then you get it done. No question we gave up a lot to get [Nathan] but we had had three really bad years and we needed a marquee player. The team needed him and our fans deserved it too. We had to have him."

And they got him. With MacKinnon and Drouin, the Mooseheads now had the top two

Nathan's 2012–13 Halifax Mooseheads card.

players from the 2011 QMJHL draft. It was the perfect recipe to help turn around a team that had fallen on hard times in recent years.

"We were incredibly excited to draft Jonathan Drouin second overall," said Russell. "To us, Drouin was an incredible player and we knew he would be an incredible player for the Mooseheads. It was an exciting time for the franchise and the city."

In acquiring MacKinnon, Russell also weighed in on the comparisons with Sidney Crosby. "He's a local kid, which is always nice, but when it's a kid of his calibre, it makes it even more exciting," Russell said in an interview with NHL.com. "[MacKinnon] is a big, strong, fast-skating power forward, great shot, great moves. They both have excellent skill sets, with Crosby being maybe more of a playmaker. But you hate to throw comparisons out there: it's not fair to the kid. He's just the best kid at his age right now."

Reaction to the trade caused a media frenzy in the Halifax hockey community. So many times over the years, the best players from Nova Scotia had left to play hockey in other provinces—Sidney Crosby being the most notable example. But rather than playing for a visiting team, MacKinnon would be coming home, and many people in his hometown were excited by the prospect.

Instead of living with a billet family in Baie-Comeau, MacKinnon was back in the house where he spent most of his childhood, back with his parents and his sister, Sarah. He was also back in the public school system. After two years at the Maritime Hockey Academy followed by two more years at Shattuck-St. Mary's, he was re-entering a traditional public school setting at Prince Andrew High School in Dartmouth, attending with several of his Mooseheads teammates, including Jonathan Drouin.

"Nathan was always a good student," said his mother, Kathy. "When he came to play for the Mooseheads, it was different [because] school was not connected to hockey. Keep in mind that Nathan attended the Maritime Hockey Academy for grades seven and eight, then went to Shattuck-St. Mary's for grades nine and ten. So hockey and school went hand in hand. Prince Andrew was very supportive in regard to the amount of time he missed. Athletes missed a lot of time so it was tough for them to stay on top of work. The school's vice-principal at time was incredibly supportive of the Mooseheads' high school players, especially Nate and Jonathan, in their grade twelve year. She worked with the two of them to ensure success."

And that success extended beyond the classroom. Even though her son was, in the eyes of many, just two years away from reaching the NHL, Nathan enjoyed a (mostly) traditional high school experience. But the demands of playing in the QMJHL denied him the moments that so many students take for granted.

"Nathan spent so little time 'hanging out' in high school that his experience was as normal as it could be. If he had an off class he would either come home or play basketball in the gym. He ran to practice right after school so there was very little time to embrace the high school experience. Hockey was always his focus."

PLAYING ON HOME ICE

In September 2011 Nathan MacKinnon came home to play permanently. Was he nervous? "A little bit," he said during training camp in the weeks leading up to his major junior hockey debut. His parents would watch him play as would his sister and his friends—but he seemed to have a breezy approach toward the upcoming challenge and pressure of playing for his hometown team.

In his Mooseheads debut on September 19, 2011, wearing number 22, MacKinnon helped pace his team with 2 assists and a shootout goal in a season-opening victory over the PEI Rocket. That opening night performance set the tone for the Mooseheads rookie, and he followed up his first QMJHL game with season-long consistency.

However, MacKinnon's solid performance in the early part of the season was not enough to earn him an invite to Canada's selection camp for the 2012 World Junior Hockey Championship. At the time, the most recent sixteen-year-old to play for Canada's junior team was Sidney Crosby in 2004, and MacKinnon's hopes of following in Crosby's footsteps were dashed in the days leading up to the tryouts.

"I guess the Canadian national program didn't feel that I was suited this year," MacKinnon said when he heard the news. "Hopefully I can go to camp next year and make the team, and do as much as I can to help the team win. I need to get better at my defensive zone play and my faceoffs. I think that will come with experience and time, but I have to improve on some of those little aspects."

Being shunned by Hockey Canada was a turning point for MacKinnon—it was an opportunity to show the hockey world that he had a rare breed of fire in the belly. If there was a highlight for him during the 2011–12 QMJHL regular season, it came the night after he found out he was not being invited to Team Canada's selection camp. That night, December 3, in a home game against the Québec Remparts, MacKinnon scored 5 goals for a 6–4 victory at the Metro Centre. "It was definitely a special night," MacKinnon said. "I don't think there's another feeling like that. When there's six or seven thousand people in the stands, standing up and cheering for you, it's a pretty special feeling and one that I'll remember for the rest of my life."

The Mooseheads' general manager Cam Russell, said considering the letdown of not being asked to try out for Team Canada, it was one of the finest on-ice performances he had ever seen. "He

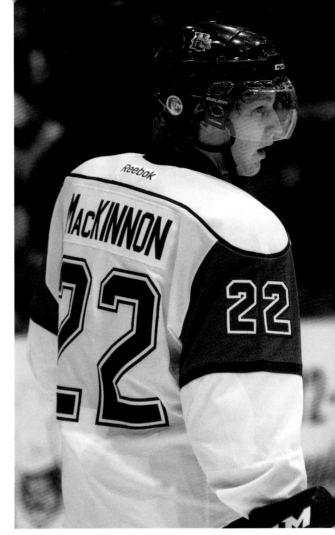

Nathan wearing #22 for the Mooseheads in a 2012 QMJHL game. THE CANADIAN PRESS / GHYSLAIN BERGERON

never said a word. He was respectable and was quiet about the decision," said Russell. "Then the next night he goes out and scores five goals against Québec! We couldn't hold the kid down. He was always out trying to prove he was the best. He was not the kind of kid to feel sorry for himself. Obstacles and disappointments just motivate him more."

Even though he had not been invited to the World Junior's selection camp, MacKinnon was not completely shunned by Hockey Canada: The sixteen-year-old MacKinnon once again represented Atlantic Canada at the 2012 World U-17 Hockey Challenge, this time held in Windsor and LaSalle, Ontario. After his stellar performance at the 2011 challenge in Manitoba, he was named team captain. Team Atlantic finished in seventh place, and MacKinnon scored 1 goal and 3 assists for a total of 4 points in 5 games.

Jon Greenwood, Nathan's teacher and coach from the Maritime Hockey Academy, remembers checking his phone that night and seeing the news on Twitter: "I just smiled and shook my head. I just thought to myself, 'of course he did that tonight.' I'm done being surprised by anything Nate does," he added. "He has proven himself to be a player who continues to get better year in, year out. I believe his competitiveness will drive him to always want to improve and I won't put a ceiling on him."

Bill Short, Hockey Nova Scotia's development coordinator, said moments like that offer a glimpse at MacKinnon's competitive edge. "It is evident when you watch Nathan play the game of hockey that he enjoys every aspect of the game," said Short. "Yes, he is competitive and does not like it when things do not go his way, but *that* is a competitor. He also has a burning desire to play the game of hockey to the fullest extent when the opportunity arises. That skill is obvious to a talent scout or an average fan. He always wants to be on ice and he always wants to play."

MacKinnon rounded out his first season of junior hockey by playing 58 games and finishing with 31 goals, 47 assists, and 78 points.

As for the Mooseheads, after three straight losing seasons, the team rebounded for an impressive 39 wins and 85 points. Crowds were up, the team's fortunes were rising, and, led by MacKinnon, they were poised to prove they were a team on the rise by heading to the playoffs. Not many expected the Mooseheads to compete for a championship in MacKinnon's rookie season, but the team entered the post-season playing some of their best hockey of the year. They had proven they were a team with all the ingredients to be a championship contender.

It wasn't just MacKinnon who was leading the team, either. After being drafted second overall but not reporting to the Mooseheads at the start of the season, Jonathan Drouin joined the team in December and played 33 regular season games, scoring 29 points. Drouin went on to add 17 points in 17 playoff games, giving the Mooseheads a dynamic duo to build their team around. Beyond MacKinnon and Drouin, other key contributors included

(L-R) Alexandre Grenier (5), Jonathan Drouin (27), Marc-Olivier Daigle (0), and Nathan MacKinnon (22) celebrate a playoff win on April 17, 2012. THE CANADIAN PRESS / JACQUES BOISSINOT

Alexandre Grenier, Darcy Ashley, Cameron Critchlow, Martin Frk, Konrad Abeltshauser, and goalie Zachary Fucale.

In the opening round of the 2012 play-offs, Halifax swept the Moncton Wildcats 4–0. In the second round, they would make history. Down three games to none to the Québec Remparts in a best-of-seven series, Halifax rallied for four straight wins to capture the series in seven games. They became the first QMJHL team to come back from a 3–0 deficit since the Cape Breton Screaming Eagles in 2001.

The Mooseheads lost the next series to the Rimouski Océanic, but as a young team on the rise, they proved that they would have a championship-calibre team the following season.

"I believe [if they] believe in themselves, that they are fairly invincible," said Hockey Nova Scotia's Bill Short. "They understand what it takes to come back and work hard as a team. They understand what it takes to win."

With Nathan MacKinnon and Jonathan Drouin anchoring, the Mooseheads were poised to take a jump to the next level. In addition to possessing world-class skill, these two young stars were also showcasing chemistry. They were drafted first and second overall in the QMJHL draft and already hockey's top scouts were speculating both players could be selected in the top five of the 2013 NHL entry draft.

MacKinnon and Drouin were friends on and off the ice; it was not uncommon to see them hanging out away from the rink during the season. On the ice, they were dynamic; they meshed immediately with their new team and gave the organization and its fans reason to be hopeful. The ever-elusive championship might finally be attainable for the Mooseheads, and soon.

2012 IVAN HLINKA MEMORIAL TOURNAMENT

MacKinnon wasn't allowed to play in the 2012 Canada-Russia Challenge because he had not been a member of Team Canada's Summer Under-18 program. Instead, he shifted his focus to prepare for the 2012 Ivan Hlinka Memorial Tournament in the Czech Republic and Slovakia in mid-August. "Obviously I am disappointed I cannot play [in the Canada-Russia Challenge]," MacKinnon told Metronews.ca. "But at the end of day, it's a one-door-closes-another-opens type of situation."

The tournament was the biggest MacKinnon had ever played, and the moment wasn't lost on him. "I've never experienced anything like this before, but it's a great way to start the season," MacKinnon said.

Team Canada won its fifth Ivan Hlinka Memorial Tournament in a row, led by MacKinnon in the gold-medal game. He scored 3 goals, two of them on power plays, and Canada defeated Finland 4–0 in the final. "They [Team Finland] don't back down. They're in your face the whole game. They wanted it bad, but I thought we just tired them out," said MacKinnon after the game. "We played good Canadian-style hockey. We're really physical, which led to our success."

MacKinnon's head coach at the tournament, Todd Gill, pointed out that many of the under-18 players would be moving up to the under-20 program to play for Canada at the World Junior Hockey Championship. "All of them, it looks like their future is bright to go forward," Gill said. "I feel really good about Hockey Canada over the next two, three years."

WORLD JUNIORS

In 2012 MacKinnon had been left off of Canada's National Junior team—that alone was a low point of his rookie season—but in 2013, not only was he considered a shoo-in to make the team, he was also being counted on to lead the team. In the end, however, the World Juniors proved to be a sour experience for MacKinnon.

Despite all the success MacKinnon enjoyed in previous Hockey Canada tournaments, his experience and performance at the 2013 World Junior Hockey Championship in Ufa, Russia, was not stellar. Team Canada struggled, and MacKinnon tallied just 1 assist over the whole tournament. Canada finished fourth, losing the bronze-medal game to host Russia, 6–5 in overtime.

Canada's Nathan MacKinnon (23) and Russia's Danil Zharkov (26) battle for the puck during bronze-medal action at the 2013 IIHF World U-20 Championship. **RICHARD WOLOWICZ / HHOF-IIHF IMAGES**

MacKinnon was expected to play a starring role at the tournament but that performance never came through. Team Canada's head coach Steve Spott used him sparingly, dropping him to the fourth line and splitting up the dynamic MacKinnon-Drouin duo that had performed so well together over two seasons with the Halifax Mooseheads. Spott faced criticism in the Canadian media for how he handled MacKinnon, and MacKinnon faced his own share of adversity: he had not performed anywhere near what everyone had expected of him. As if to rub salt in the wound, the team did not perform well overall. Whenever Canada's national junior team fails to win gold, people ask some tough questions and some critics laid the heat on MacKinnon—especially in the days immediately after the tournament ended.

"That was a tough situation to watch. I could see the frustration on his face on TV," said Nathan's former coach and teacher Jon Greenwood. "I think that was the only time

MACKINNON AND DROUIN

Nathan MacKinnon and Jonathan Drouin didn't know each other very well before becoming teammates on the Mooseheads. They had played against each other, most recently at the 2011 Canada Winter Games in Halifax (Drouin for Team Québec, MacKinnon for Team Nova Scotia), but the seeds of friendship were sown in the weeks and months leading up to the time when they became teammates.

"Not only Moosehead teammates, they went to school and drove each day together," said Nathan's mother Kathy. "They experienced the World Juniors together and of course enjoyed the NHL draft journey together. It was a special bond for sure that will always continue. They keep in touch when they can through a very busy schedule and made sure to put time aside in each of their home cities when their teams arrived in town."

Mooseheads general manager Cam Russell remembered MacKinnon and Drouin becoming fast friends both on and off the ice "I think they were good for each other. It's difficult to be a player of that calibre and be that young. They helped each other, pushed each other, and were heavy competitors with each other." Their competition was good-natured, with a foundation of friendship that allowed both players to thrive in their junior surroundings together, as equals. "They'd spend all day at the rink trying to improve then I'd see them jumping in the car and driving home together," said Russell. "Their friendship played a big role in our championship season and it's one of my great memories of that year."

in his life, including later as a NHL rookie, that he did not play a prominent role on his team. I was just a fan, I have no idea what the dynamics were like over there in Russia. But I felt for him and could sense the frustration."

MacKinnon handled the heat with grace: "We didn't want the finish we had, but it was definitely a great experience," he said. When asked if he thought the team's performance might impact the upcoming NHL draft in June, he said, "I don't think so. I think the scouts and GMs know what kind of players we are. Obviously I wanted to play more, but it's not about me. No complaints. In the NHL—hopefully I will get there one day—I know I won't always be the go-to guy every time. This was definitely a good experience for me and a good change and I think I will take the positives from it."

While MacKinnon was clearly disappointed in his own play, he was outwardly happy for his friend and Mooseheads teammate Jonathan Drouin, who played 6 games for Canada and scored 2 goals with 2 assists and was +4 overall in the tournament.

"I think he just carried his play from the season to the world juniors," said MacKinnon, speaking with reporters at Halifax Stanfield International Airport upon his return from the World Juniors in Russia. "He didn't change too much in his game…I'm really happy for him and he's going to help us in the second half of the [QMJHL] season."

THE 4 PRESIDENT CUP

The 2012–13 season held unprecedented promise for the Halifax Mooseheads: many hoped they would break through and finally win their first QMJHL championship in franchise history. The talent had been assembled and, based on the team's play the previous season, many fans expected them to crank it up one more notch. Maybe they could win a QMJHL championship...maybe even a Memorial Cup.

Not only was this clearly the best Mooseheads team ever assembled, it would also prove to be one of most successful single-season team performances in major junior hockey history.

During the regular season, the Mooseheads were dominant. It seemed like they never lost, winning 58 of 68 games played. They lost only 6 games in regulation time and 4 games in overtime for a total of just 10 losses in 68 games—very close to setting an all-time record for junior hockey excellence.

Jonathan Drouin led the team in scoring, with 41 goals and 105 points in just 49 regular season games played. But beyond MacKinnon and Drouin, the Mooseheads had vast

CHL FEWEST LOSSES IN ONE SEASON

▷ 5 Brandon Wheat Kings, WHL, 1978–79 (72 games)

▷ 7 Québec Remparts, QMJHL, 1970–71 (62 games)

▷ 7 Toronto Marlboros, OHL, 1972–73 (63 games)

stores of elite talent. Martin Frk contributed 84 points in 56 games. Darcy Ashley, Matthew Boudreau, Stefan Fournier, and Luca Ciampini all chipped in with at least 70 points each. Stephen MacAulay, Trey Lewis, and Ryan Falkenham provided key contributions, and Konrad Abeltshauser would seal his reputation as a dominant junior defenceman. Goalie Zachary Fucale would win 45 of the 53 games he played in nets, with a .909 save percentage and two shutouts. The 2012–13 Mooseheads had it all.

The regular season was proving to be a historically successful one for the Mooseheads. They were winning most nights and Drouin and MacKinnon were on track to finish well above the 100-point mark during the regular season. But as good as the season was for Halifax, the year included another moment of adversity for seventeen-year-old MacKinnon when he suffered a knee injury in February 2013.

In the hockey world, teams are often vague about players' injuries, lest they reveal possible vulnerabilities, and the Mooseheads were no different. They called MacKinnon's setback a "lower-body injury."

In this case, "lower-body" meant knee.

MacKinnon had injured his medial collateral ligament, or MCL, which is one of the knee's four major ligaments. It was a relatively minor injury, but it still caused a headache for the player and his team. It sidelined MacKinnon for several weeks, depriving the Mooseheads of their best player at a critical time in the season. "Hopefully I have a long career ahead of me and I don't think a minor MCL injury will hurt it at all," said MacKinnon. "I think, right now, it's not worth making it worse and putting a long playoff run in jeopardy."

But while MacKinnon played it down, reaction to the injury quickly became headline news in hockey circles. "I kind of laugh about it now," said MacKinnon. "I'm out for six to seven days and it's all over Twitter. This type of injury is not going to hurt my [NHL] draft at all."

The injury gave MacKinnon a chance to rest during a long hockey season, but with the fast-approaching NHL entry draft, it could have been bad timing. Since he was not playing and there was a level of uncertainty surrounding his health, some people argued that MacKinnon's draft stock could drop: he was already in a shortlisted contest to see which player would be drafted number one overall.

Mooseheads Head Coach Dominique Ducharme wasn't worried, since the scouts had seen MacKinnon play a lot since the previous year. "They saw him play thirty to forty times. They know what kind of player he is. They want to see how you handle adversity," said Ducharme.

The knee injury also dramatically altered MacKinnon's point total for the season. The injury, combined with his time away while playing at the World Junior Hockey Championship in Russia,

Nathan MacKinnon (22) checks Jeremie Malouin of the Québec Remparts during the 2012 QMJHL playoffs.

limited MacKinnon to just 44 regular games by the end of the season. While he managed to score 32 goals and add 43 assists for a total of 75 points over those 44 games, he fell to fifth place on the team for scoring—far below his pre-season expectations.

2013 QMJHL PLAYOFFS

The Mooseheads began the 2013 playoffs by facing the two-time defending QMJHL champions and 2011 Memorial Cup champions the Saint John Sea Dogs in the opening round. It wasn't even close. Halifax set the tone early by winning the first game 9–1 on

QMJHL 2012–13 REGULAR SEASON STANDINGS

	Team	Wins	Losses	Points
EAST DIVISION	Baie-Comeau Drakkar	37	19	93
	Rimouski Océanic	33	18	91
	Québec Remparts	33	21	89
	Victoriaville Tigres	26	27	73
	Chicoutimi Saguenéens	25	31	67
	Shawinigan Cataractes	11	46	37
	Team	**Wins**	**Losses**	**Points**
WEST DIVISION	Blainville-Boisbriand Armada	40	19	90
	Rouyn-Noranda Huskies	32	24	84
	Drummondville Voltigeurs	28	26	80
	Val-d'Or Foreurs	30	27	76
	Gatineau Olympiques	23	34	63
	Sherbrooke Phoenix	14	38	51
	Team	**Wins**	**Losses**	**Points**
MARITIMES DIVISION	Halifax Mooseheads	53	6	120
	Moncton Wildcats	36	23	87
	Charlottetown Islanders	37	23	86
	Acadie-Bathurst Titan	21	35	59
	Saint John Sea Dogs	15	44	47
	Cape Breton Screaming Eagles	13	46	36

home ice. They went on to sweep the series in four straight games with a combined score of 25–4.

MacKinnon finished the series with an impressive 7 points in 4 games, but players and coaches alike agreed it was an all-around team effort. Halifax's star players made key contributions in the series but many of the Mooseheads' unheralded players also played pivotal roles in the victory.

On April 5, 2013, the Mooseheads began their second-round series against the Gatineau Olympiques, a team that finished 57 points behind them in the regular season standings. Just like the opening round against Saint John, this was a short series.

The Mooseheads came out flying and won 7–0. MacKinnon didn't score, but he did contribute 4 assists. "It was a really good start," MacKinnon said. "We got a couple of power play goals and we just kind of cruised from there. There were a couple times in the game we could've been better; we had some little mental lapses. But I think we're going to feed off this victory and hopefully get it going tomorrow again."

Halifax took game two 5–0 with goaltender Zachary Fucale performing 13 saves to secure another shutout. Back-to-back shutouts are a rarity, especially in the playoffs, and the significance of this feat was not lost on the Mooseheads' net-minder. "It's a lot of fun," Fucale said. "I think the whole team is cherishing it. It's not just me at all. We were all proud of get-ting a shutout. A shutout is never just the goalie. There's always something behind it and I think the boys had a huge part in that game tonight."

With two convincing home wins under their belt, the Mooseheads were just two more wins away from reaching the QMJHL semifinal. They were making fast work of their opponents, and the team that domi-nated the regular season was looking just as dominant in the playoffs.

Game three in Gatineau was much closer. Halifax ultimately prevailed 4–2, but the scoreboard was close for the first time in the playoffs, and the Mooseheads were forced to hold until the dying seconds. An

Nathan during a game against the Rimouski Océanic on November 20, 2012. THE CANADIAN PRESS / REMI SENECHAL

empty-net goal from Stefan Fournier with 14.2 seconds left clinched the win for Halifax.

Game four was another close one, and once again it took an empty-net goal to seal the victory. Jonathan Drouin scored on the empty net with 27 seconds left in the third period and the Mooseheads won 5–3 to sweep the Olympiques in four straight games.

"We knew it would be tough coming in to this building but I think we reacted well to the adversity we had to face here," said Mooseheads forward Stephen MacAulay. "It maybe wasn't our prettiest game but I'm just glad to have it over with."

HOME ICE HEARTBREAK

In 2000 the Mooseheads hosted the CHL Memorial Cup final and watched as the Océanic, led by Brad Richards of Murray Harbour, Prince Edward Island, won the championship at the Metro Centre on their home ice. Richards went on to lead the Tampa Bay Lightning to a Stanley Cup victory and win the Conn Smythe Trophy as the NHL's most valuable player in the 2004 Stanley Cup playoffs.

One year later, in 2005, Sidney Crosby led the Océanic to the QMJHL President Cup with a four-game series sweep over the Mooseheads—with the series-clinching game hosted in Halifax.

Two historic wins by the Océanic and two tough setbacks for the Mooseheads and their fans. It's safe to say the Mooseheads wanted to stop the trend in 2013.

In the series-clinching win, MacKinnon had 2 assists, and after the game he used the moment to compliment team captain Stefan Fournier, who led the way with 3 goals. "It's awesome," said MacKinnon. "That guy has had an up and down QMJHL career. He broke his leg twice. But with his compete level and his strength he's a typical playoff player. It's a really cool story for him…he's a great captain and he leads by example. It's great to see a guy like that really succeed."

The Mooseheads' next step was the Rouyn-Noranda Huskies and the QMJHL semifinal. The winner would advance to the President Cup league championship.

The first game of the series was April 20 at the Metro Centre in Halifax. The Mooseheads squandered two separate 2-goal leads, but emerged with a 6–4 win in the final period. MacKinnon led the way with 3 goals in front of a jam-packed home crowd of more than 10,500 fans.

Healthy and rested, MacKinnon was the dominant player many expected him to be. He was skating faster than he had during the regular season, and was playing a heavy and tough game. The addition of more physicality came at just the right time because the Huskies were proving to be a difficult opponent. "It's not a surprise at all," said Jonathan Drouin to a group of reporters after posting 5 points for Halifax in game one. "We knew coming into the series they have a really good team. They surprised Québec [in the second round] for a reason."

Game two was even closer, and Halifax trailed for the first two periods before scoring twice in the third to send the game to sudden death overtime. A power play goal by Martin Frk decided Halifax's 5–4 victory.

The Mooseheads line of Frk, MacKinnon, and Drouin combined for 11 points in game two alone, and the team pulled out a gutsy win to take a 2–0 series lead.

Nathan celebrating a goal against the Québec Remparts during a game on April 6, 2012. THE CANADIAN PRESS / JACQUES BOISSINOT

"I think that's just the way it goes sometimes," said MacKinnon, who assisted the winning goal. "They have a pretty fast team and at times we were playing a lot of hockey so maybe there was a little fatigue for a while. I don't know what it was but I thought we really wore them down, especially on the tying goal. Their D looked like they couldn't even stand up. It was little stuff like that that helped us out. We have so much depth and it's awesome when different guys step up."

Game three was just as close and dramatic, and ultimately the pivotal game for Halifax. The Mooseheads led early 1–0 and were up 2–1 in the third when the Huskies tied the game with only 3:52 left to go in regulation time.

But in the extra time, MacKinnon once again assisted a game-winning goal, this one by Jonathan Drouin. The Mooseheads now had a stronghold on the series and were just one win away from advancing to the President Cup final for the third time in the franchise's history.

It seemed that MacKinnon's injury was healed, allowing the young star to play at his top level at the most crucial juncture of his career. His speed was explosive and his physical play was as strong as ever. Even though he was younger than many of his opponents, he never shied away from the rougher elements of the game. After his frustrating knee injury held him to just 75 points in 44 regular season games, he was now producing offensively at an astonishing rate and he finished the QMJHL playoffs with 33 points in 17 games—a scoring pace that, if pro-rated, would put him in the vicinity of 150 points over the course of a regular season.

JUNIOR HOCKEY HOTBED

Halifax was once considered a lousy hockey market when it came to fan support. During the 2003 IIHF World Junior Hockey Championship, Team Canada's head coach Marc Habscheid was asked about his memories playing in Halifax for the Nova Scotia Oilers of the American Hockey League in 1984–85. In those days, the Oilers drew 2,500–3,500 fans in a 9,200-seat Metro Centre (which has since been expanded to 10,500). Habscheid's recollection was of the venue's many "empty orange seats."

Before the Oilers, the Nova Scotia Voyageurs were considered a flagship franchise in the AHL and won three Calder Cups in the 1970s. Those teams packed the Halifax Forum in the playoffs, but in the regular season, even the dominant "Vees" rarely drew more than three thousand fans per game.

When the QMJHL expansion franchise was announced for Halifax, it was considered a risk given the sometimes-tepid fan support in Halifax—especially at the Metro Centre. But, from the team's inception in 1994, the Mooseheads have consistently drawn more than seven thousand fans per game during both the playoffs and regular season.

The 2003 World Junior Hockey Championship further augmented Halifax's reputation by setting new records for attendance and profit. The Halifax-Sydney tandem host city drew a whopping 242,173 people and hauled in more than $3.5 million.

"There is no question that the host committees of Halifax and Sydney hosted an extremely successful event, achieving record attendance, record television ratings, and record profits," said Hockey Canada president Bob Nicholson. "Our hats go off to the hundreds of volunteers who dedicated their time and effort prior to and during last year's World Juniors, and thank you to hockey fans across Canada for their support of the event."

After years of slowly proving that Halifax could draw numbers, the Mooseheads' postseason attendance records from the spring of 2013 finally cemented the city's standing as a "good draw" hockey city.

Nathan MacKinnon was impossible to defend or contain, and was playing the best hockey of his life at a time when his team needed him more than ever. As TSN Hockey Insider Bob McKenzie put it, MacKinnon was showing the world that he was a young star capable of dominating the game in all areas. "Nathan MacKinnon has all the tools—dynamic speed and power, strength, and most importantly, elite level skill—to skate his way into the pantheon of NHL superstars. He's one of those players who, as soon as he gets the puck on his stick and takes off, there's a palpable sense of excitement and anticipation at what's going to happen next."

Halifax Mooseheads General Manager Cam Russell suggested MacKinnon's regular-season knee injury might be the main reason he was playing so well in the post-season. "It was a blessing in disguise," said Russell. "When you look at players like Nathan, you don't want them to be winning scoring titles and have nothing left in tank and lose in the first round of the playoffs. He came into the playoffs rested and he was flying. He had played so much and was so good [in the regular season], but it had taken a toll. The injury allowed him to rest and refocus and it really showed in his play."

The first three games of the series were tough, dramatic affairs, but the fourth and final game was not close. For a while the Huskies kept pace—it was 4–4 in the second period—but the Mooseheads exploded for 3 straight goals in the third period, for a 9–6 win and yet another series sweep.

"It's pretty cool going to the finals. It's been our goal all year and it's here now," said MacKinnon, who had 2 goals and 2 assists in game four. "We're really looking forward to the challenge. We blew through the first couple of rounds. We won some really close games in this series. We're confident no matter what the situation, we'll come through."

The Mooseheads were a dominating 12–0 in the playoffs and were now primed to face the Baie-Comeau Drakkar. The Drakkar, thanks to their consistent fan support, bigger arena, and propensity for producing star players, were the epitome of junior hockey excellence. It would be an uphill battle, but the Mooseheads were poised for their first ever league title, and were just four wins away from advancing to the CHL Memorial Cup playoffs for the first time in the team's history. And this time, unlike Halifax's two previous President Cup appearances, the Mooseheads were favoured to win.

MacKinnon, Drouin, and Frk had 101 combined points in the post-season—Drouin with 35, Frk and MacKinnon with 33 each. The team was firing on all cylinders. The young stars and the players were performing at their highest levels, and at the most opportune time.

PRESIDENT CUP FINAL

The Halifax Mooseheads' opponent in the QMJHL championship final was the Baie-Comeau Drakkar, the team MacKinnon refused to play for when he was drafted the previous season. "It's kind of funny that we're playing those guys in the final with everything that's happened," MacKinnon told the Halifax *Chronicle-Herald* before game one. "I know it's going to be a storyline, and I'm sure some people will be talking about it, but we're just looking forward to getting things going."

MacKinnon was also braced for any negative reaction from the Drakkar fans who were unhappy that he had asked to be traded just days after being drafted. "I don't know what's going to happen but I'm sure [...] their fans are going to have fun with it and that's fine." MacKinnon said. "They have emotional fans and they're into their hockey and there's nothing wrong with that."

MacKinnon also used the lead-up to the series to clarify his reasons for not going to Baie-Comeau. "I got advice about where I could go and what would be best for me," MacKinnon said. "I was fifteen years old and I had a lot of different options I could pursue, so I wanted to look at all of them at the time. But I think the way everything's worked out, I'm having a great time in Halifax. I love being able to live at home and be with my family. This is a really special

hockey club and I think I've developed well as a player the last two years."

The series began on May 3, 2013, at the Metro Centre. For the first game, in a frenzied playoff atmosphere, the Mooseheads came out flying with high energy and grabbed the opener 4–0, and stretched their playoff winning streak to fourteen games.

Game two was closer and more dramatic. Halifax won 4–3 and MacKinnon chipped in with 1 assist in a game that appeared closer on the scoreboard than it was on the ice. But more important than the individual victory, the Mooseheads were in command of the series—up 2–0.

Games three and four were played in Baie-Comeau and Halifax had a chance to

THE NOVA SCOTIA VOYAGEURS AND THE CALDER CUP

The American Hockey League's Nova Scotia Voyageurs were a dominant franchise in the 1970s, winning three championships (1971–72, 1975–76, and 1976–77) while calling Halifax their home city and the Forum their home arena.

The Vees moved their games from the Forum to the Metro Centre in 1978, and eventually left Halifax and moved to Sherbrooke, Québec, in 1984. Halifax went thirty-six years before winning another major hockey championship (excluding junior A titles).

METRO CENTRE ATTENDANCE, 2013 PLAYOFFS

Date	Opponent	Attendance
March 22	Saint John	9,120
March 23	Saint John	9,551
April 5	Gatineau	9,895
April 6	Gatineau	10,242
April 20	Rouyn-Noranda	10,595
April 21	Rouyn-Noranda	10,138
May 3	Baie-Comeau	10,595
May 4	Baie-Comeau	10,595
May 10	Baie-Comeau	10,595

2013 home playoff attendance total: 91,326

sweep the series in four games, but those dreams were short-lived: the Drakkar won game three 3–1, letting Halifax know that they were a force to be reckoned with. "[Game three] was a tight game," Mooseheads Head Coach Dominique Ducharme said. "We knew this series was going to be a battle. With that win tonight, they showed that. There are some things we can do better and we'll concentrate on doing that tomorrow."

The Mooseheads offence came alive in game four, and Halifax won 7–4. MacKinnon had 1 goal and 1 assist, Frk had 2 goals and 3 assists, and Drouin had 1 goal and 3 assists. Halifax's best players led the way and helped put the franchise one win away from hoisting their first President Cup: an

opportunity that had only knocked once before. In 2000, when Halifax was hosting the tournament, the team was automatically awarded a berth to the final. This was different. This was a battle hard-won.

PRESIDENT CUP FINAL: GAME FIVE

On May 10, 2013, the Metro Centre was filled to capacity: 10,595 people crammed in to watch game five. They came to witness a championship on home ice and they did not leave the arena disappointed. The game was virtually over within minutes. Halifax jumped out to a 3–0 first-period lead and

Nathan lifting the 2013 President Cup after defeating the Baie-Comeau Drakkar in the Halifax Metro Centre on May 10, 2013. THE CANADIAN PRESS / ANDREW VAUGHAN

did not let up, on the way to an historic 5-1 victory. This was MacKinnon's final season with the Mooseheads—it was expected that he would be playing in the NHL in October—and he was beaming ear-to-ear as his team hoisted the QMJHL championship trophy on home ice.

The Metro Centre has been the venue for many loud and boisterous occasions. During Team Canada's home games for the 2003 World Junior Hockey Championship, the arena was arguably louder than ever before. But many who witnessed the Mooseheads' 2013 championship-clinching game said the Metro Centre on that night—especially during the dying minutes of the third period—said it was the loudest ever in the history of the arena. It was also the first major championship won at the Metro Centre. Not counting CIS Men's Basketball Championships, no champion had ever been crowned at the Metro Centre.

"It's been a long time coming for everybody," said MacKinnon after winning the game. "It's definitely one of the best feelings of my life and I can guarantee it's the same for every one of my teammates."

THE **5** MEMORIAL CUP

With the President Cup victory, the Mooseheads were off to Saskatoon, Saskatchewan, for their second Memorial Cup appearance in team history. Their opponents in the round robin format included two-time Memorial Cup champions the Portland Winterhawks, 2005 Memorial Cup champions the London Knights, and the host team, the Saskatoon Blades, who had yet to win the cup.

MacKinnon set the pace for Halifax in the opening game by scoring 3 goals, and the Mooseheads beat Portland 7–4. The game featured Canada's three top-ranked players leading into the 2013 NHL entry draft: MacKinnon, his teammate Jonathan Drouin, and Portland defenceman Seth Jones.

Among the three, MacKinnon stood out most in the opening game. "I thought I had a pretty slow first period, but the next forty minutes I thought we controlled the play," said MacKinnon. "I think we deserved the win."

(L-R) Nathan MacKinnon, Seth Jones, and Jonathan Drouin after a press conference in Saskatoon, Saskatchewan, on May 16, 2013. THE CANADIAN PRESS / LIAM RICHARDS

MACKINNON AND JONES

Seth Jones and Nathan MacKinnon, just like other QMJHL rivals Connor McDavid and Jack Eichel or Tyler Seguin and Taylor Hall, were linked prior to their final junior season. In the days following the 2012 NHL entry draft, MacKinnon and Jones were immediately billed as favourites to be the top two picks in the 2013 draft, although there was disagreement over who would be picked first and which player was the better of the two. Jones, being a defenceman, had different skills than MacKinnon, who was speedy power forward.

By the time the draft came around in June 2013, the two had become friends. They faced off in the 2013 Top Prospects Game, an annual showcase of the CHL's top forty

(L-R) Seth Jones, Nathan MacKinnon, and Jonathan Drouin. THE CANADIAN PRESS / LIAM RICHARDS

NHL draft-eligible players. Jones emerged victorious that game, but four months later, he fell to MacKinnon and the Mooseheads in the Memorial Cup final. Jones's draft status plummeted, and he went from a lock to be first or second overall, to being selected forth.

The Mooseheads had momentum, but it was stalled in the second game against the host team, the Saskatoon Blades. MacKinnon scored another goal, but his team lost (for just the second time in the post-season) 5–2 to the Blades.

"We're going to have to scratch and claw to win this," Moosehead forward Stephen MacAulay said after the game in an interview with the *Chronicle-Herald*. "We were really excited to beat Portland, who we knew were a top team all year, and maybe we weren't focused right off the hop. It's a quick turnaround to play the host team

right after, it's pretty tough. We didn't have a good start again."

MacKinnon had a similar outlook: "We had a good ten to twelve minutes and that's not enough," he said in an interview with the *Chronicle-Herald*. "We had opportunities to get a couple late and we didn't bury them. We've got to do that. If you score earlier, it's a different game."

The Mooseheads rebounded the next night by thumping the London Knights 9–2. Halifax's dynamic duo, forwards MacKinnon and Drouin, each collected 3 assists.

The Mooseheads finished the Memorial Cup round robin with a 2–1 record and earned a bye into the final where, once again, their opponents would be the Portland Winterhawks: Nathan MacKinnon versus Seth Jones.

Major junior hockey supremacy was on the line and so, perhaps, was the top spot at the upcoming NHL entry draft.

MEMORIAL CUP FINAL

In the final game the Halifax Mooseheads, led by MacKinnon, came out strong. As a team, they continued their hot streak with 6 goals, 3 by MacKinnon—including a dramatic empty-net goal—to seal the 6–4 win over Portland.

Throughout his entire amateur career, MacKinnon's coaches and teammates had counted on him to lead in crucial game situations. The Memorial Cup final was no different. In the final sixty seconds of the third period, the Portland Winterhawks were trailing 5–4. The team pulled their goalie and added an extra skater to try and tie the game.

MacKinnon—as expected—was on the ice in his final shift as a junior hockey player, and made it one of the strongest shifts of his career. With twenty-three seconds left to go, he let fly a shot that landed in Portland's empty net. It was his final goal as

a junior, and it clinched the Memorial Cup for his team.

After the game, amid the celebration on ice, MacKinnon told the Halifax *Chronicle-Herald* that his empty-net goal to seal the victory was the biggest of his young career. "I might not score a bigger goal in my life," he said. "The empty-netter will be in my mind forever. It's unbelievable. I grew up in Halifax. I've watched this team go through hard times and good times. After that second period, there was a little doubt creeping into our minds but at the same time we had a pretty solid third period. They made it close again but it's all worth it. I don't know if we'll ever see a team like that in junior again. We had one of the best winning percentages ever in junior hockey. That was a pretty special year."

MacKinnon and Drouin had 5 points each in the championship game. For Mooseheads General Manager Cam Russell, the performance from his two best players validated all of the hard work and risk (through trades) that it took to bring them both to Halifax. "Nathan is a big-game player," said Russell. "Look at that final. Big players have to be your big players. Both Drouin and Nathan had five points each in the final game. That's why we won."

Russell also said the performance by MacKinnon was especially notable given the adversity he had faced at such a young age. "So many kids would crumble under the pressure that he faces every day," he

Nathan celebrating a third-period goal at the Memorial Cup final in Saskatoon, Saskatchewan on May 26, 2013.
THE CANADIAN PRESS / LIAM RICHARDS

explained. "He handled it and he's always handled it. He's incredible, always talking to the press and always elevating his game to the next level. And remember, at the Memorial Cup, in the playoffs, and all season long, he was always playing against the best players in the game. The other teams don't put their sixth or seventh defencemen on Nathan. They put their best on him and he handles it well."

In the stands that night sat Nathan's family, cheering him on as they had for more than a decade. The MacKinnons had witnessed the young player's success many times, but this was different: the Memorial Cup was a closing chapter in Nathan's pre-NHL career. It was an emotional thrill for his mother, Kathy, his father, Graham, and his sister, Sarah.

"The QMJHL championship in front of a home crowd, in your city, winning that title was amazing for those boys," said Kathy. "I remember thinking at the time, 'just getting to the Memorial Cup is amazing in

Nathan lifting the Memorial Cup after defeating the Portland Winterhawks on May 26, 2013.
THE CANADIAN PRESS / LIAM RICHARDS

itself.' And to think those boys won it—it still makes us pinch ourselves. You realize how difficult it is to play each and every game and to see them be the ones left standing in the end was again, surreal. Going to Saskatoon as a family to see this tournament was a special moment in time. This was an amazing year of hockey to watch and a very special group of boys who will always be connected by the Memorial Cup win."

The win also capped a four-year rebuilding project led by Mooseheads General

A huge crowd greets the CHL champion Mooseheads at the Halifax Stanfield Airport on May 27, 2013.

THE CANADIAN PRESS / ANDREW VAUGHAN

Manager Cam Russell. He had drafted and traded for stars like Fucale, MacKinnon, and Drouin. After suffering through some lean years at the bottom of the QMJHL standings, the trades, the gambles, and the hard work had paid off. "To bring the Memorial Cup to Halifax is something that was just a dream four years ago for us when we started this," Russell said. "Mission accomplished. It's an incredible feeling."

2013 MEMORIAL CUP ROUND ROBIN STANDINGS

Team	Games	W	L	Goals for	Goals Against
Halifax Mooseheads (QMJHL)	3	2	1	18	11
Portland Winterhawks (WHL)	3	2	1	14	12
London Knights (OHL)	3	1	2	8	17
Saskatoon Blades (Host/WHL)	3	1	2	9	9

6
2013 NHL ENTRY DRAFT

Having hockey players from Nova Scotia highly ranked heading into the NHL entry draft isn't a new phenomenon, but it's hardly a common occurrence. The most notable example from recent history is Al MacInnis, who was drafted in 1982. MacInnis was selected fifteenth overall by the Calgary Flames and went on to become one of the best NHL defencemen of all time. Inducted into the Hockey Hall of Fame in 2007, MacInnis won a Stanley Cup with the Flames in 1989 and also scored 1,274 points in 1,416 NHL regular-season games. Winner of the Norris Trophy for the league's top defenceman in 1999, MacInnis's best statistical season came in 1990–91 when he totaled 103 points, finishing the season with a +42 in plus/minus ratings. He also had the NHL's hardest slapshot for most of his career. Until the mid-2000s, MacInnis was widely considered to be the top Nova Scotia NHL player of all time—until Sidney Crosby burst onto the scene.

Three days before the NHL draft, Nathan MacKinnon's mother, Kathy, along with some family and friends, stood curbside at LaGuardia Airport in New York City looking for a taxi into the city. Nathan was *the* story leading into the draft; at seventeen, he was arguably the best teenaged hockey player in the world, and he was seventy-two hours away from (potentially) being selected number one overall. Kathy, though, was all smiles, fully soaking in the moment. "We'd never been to New York and here we were—our son (and brother) was

41

AL MACINNIS INDUCTION SPEECH AT THE HOCKEY HALL OF FAME IN TORONTO, 2007:

Hockey has given me something I wouldn't otherwise have: the opportunity, the challenges, lessons, rewards, responsibility, friendship, and most importantly, family. Hockey has brought me here this evening to the Hockey Hall of Fame to accept an award that is simply unimaginable. My life's journey has been blessed and I thank my family and friends, the game of hockey, and the good Lord for my continued good fortune. With that, my final thought this evening is a tribute to where this wonderful journey began forty-four years ago. To the people of Nova Scotia: you were my neighbours, my classmates, my relatives, my friends. You were good people. To represent you as the first person ever from Nova Scotia to be inducted into the Hockey Hall of Fame is a privilege of the highest degree. My place in this Hall is your place as well.

being drafted to go to the NHL!" she said, remembering the tension and excitement of the three-day journey. "The NHL draft was always mentioned in our house like the year you graduate high school. I think Nathan was seven years old when he did the math that 2013 was *his* year. When 2013 finally arrived, it was a blur. Coming off a Memorial Cup win, then off to an NHL draft was more than parents could imagine. Nathan was living his dream and what more could Graham and I ask for?"

There was speculation that defenceman Seth Jones might get picked first overall, but in the weeks leading into the draft, and most notably with his play at the Memorial Cup, MacKinnon had cemented his status as the most likely number-one pick.

"What makes Nathan stand out is that he has a real quickness with his read and react: his hockey sense, how he sees the ice, and his vision," said Dan Marr, director of NHL Central Scouting. "That is something special in a player. He is continuing to physically mature, but already he's got a lot of grit in his game and he is a competitive player."

On the day before the draft, MacKinnon and the other top prospects Jonathan Drouin, Seth Jones, Max Domi, Aleksander Barkov, and Sean Monahan, were part of a media session at an outdoor venue along the Jersey Shore. It was stiflingly hot. A swarm of reporters crushed up against MacKinnon and his fellow hockey prospects, but MacKinnon was patient, poised, and, to all outward appearances, not nervous.

(L-R) NHL prospects Zachary Fucale, Darnell Nurse, Aleksander Barkov, Nathan MacKinnon, Jonathan Drouin, Seth Jones, Sean Monahan, and Hunter Shinkaruk in New York City on June 28, 2013. THE CANADIAN PRESS / NEIL DAVIDSON

His mother, Kathy, said in an interview with *Metro News*, "Hockey is who he is. I know it might sound hokey, but it is what he wants to do." Most seventeen-year-olds struggle with making oral presentations in high school classrooms, but here was Nathan MacKinnon: handling the media and its constant glare with deftness and maturity. He talked about how he hoped to "sleep in late" on draft day and how he was also cheering for Seth Jones, the top-ranked defensive prospect.

In his blog on NHL.com, MacKinnon stressed that he was open to playing anywhere. "I'm still rooming with Seth Jones;

there's no competitive nature between us. We've talked about the top pick, but no matter where we go, it's going to be an unbelievable experience. Both of us want to begin our careers and it doesn't matter where that is…I just want to have fun and get the day going."

DRAFT DAY: JUNE 30, 2013

In 2013 the NHL entry draft was compressed into one day rather than the traditional two-day affair, and it rolled by at

(L-R) Colorado Avalanche Head Coach Patrick Roy, first overall draft pick Nathan MacKinnon, and Executive VP of Operations Joe Sakic on June 30, 2013. ASSOCIATED PRESS / BILL KOSTROUN

lightning speed. When NHL commissioner Gary Bettman took to the podium to begin the draft, he summoned the Colorado Avalanche front office and coaching staff to the stage to make the first selection within minutes. Seconds later, Avalanche Executive Vice-President of Operations Joe Sakic made the choice that most people were expecting: "The Colorado Avalanche are proud to select with our first pick, from the Halifax Mooseheads, Nathan MacKinnon."

As the cameras focused on MacKinnon, sitting next to his father, Graham, he seemed to squirm in his seat. Perhaps, finally, he was a bit nervous after all.

Moments later when MacKinnon answered reporters' questions in a room under the stands at Newark's Prudential Center, he admitted to being overwhelmed by the experience: "I kind of blacked out for a second, but it's so cool," he said. "They have such a promising team and such good

Nathan MacKinnon's Twitter reaction to being selected first overall:

So proud to be part of the @Avalanche organization!!!

MacKinnon tweeted to more than 45,000 Twitter followers. His following has since swelled to more than 130,000.

TOP FIVE DRAFT PICKS—2013 NHL ENTRY DRAFT

1. Nathan MacKinnon, Centre (Colorado Avalanche)
2. Aleksander Barkov, Jr., Centre (Florida Panthers)
3. Jonathan Drouin, Left Wing (Tampa Bay Lightning)
4. Seth Jones, Defense (Nashville Predators)
5. Elias Lindholm, Centre (Carolina Hurricanes)

(Top-bottom) Nathan MacKinnon, Aleksander Barkov, and Jonathan Drouin.
ASSOCIATED PRESS / BILL KOSTROUN

young talent, and hopefully I can be a part of that. I was definitely more nervous than I expected to be a couple of minutes before the draft."

Nathan wasn't the only one who "blacked out," or at least got temporarily lost in the euphoria of the moment. "A blur in time," said Kathy. "We both wanted to rewind and do it again so we could process the moment. To say it was overwhelming is an understatement. To see our son's dream unfold before our eyes was amazing, truly amazing!"

Growing up, MacKinnon had always admired Joe Sakic as a player, and hearing his childhood idol draft him into the NHL was surreal. "Coming from Joe Sakic's mouth, it was special," said MacKinnon. "Joe retired when I was young but I got to see him win a Stanley Cup. He was such a great leader. I've got to know him a little bit more, and I can tell why he was captain for all of those years. I was for sure a Colorado

fan first. I'm not going to lie, but I switched to Pittsburgh. I hopped on that bandwagon. But for the first part of my life, I was an Avs fan and I guess it's a little ironic that now I am here."

MacKinnon was also excited to play for Avalanche rookie head coach Patrick Roy, who had coached against MacKinnon for the Québec Remparts in the QMJHL. "I'm pretty familiar with [Roy]," MacKinnon said. "I know his systems pretty well, just from studying against him in the playoffs. I'm not sure if they're going to be the same or not, but I know his style. He's a very competitive guy, and his will to win is second to none, so I'm very excited to play for him."

Even with all the hype of draft day, it was not lost on MacKinnon that he was able to share the moment with his family. "It was a great moment for my friends and family to be there and I got to celebrate when I came back [to Nova Scotia] as well," he said. "They've meant everything. They're my biggest supporters and biggest fans. They've experienced everything with me. They travelled to the Memorial Cup. They came to the draft. They were there all through my minor hockey. It's been a great run. You need a strong family to be able to do everything I've done."

MacKinnon also shared the moment with someone who had become as close as any family member: his former minor hockey coach and teacher, Jon Greenwood. Greenwood was invited to Newark to watch the draft with the MacKinnon family and spent the post-draft festivities with his former player. "It was a special moment

FIRST OVERALL NHL DRAFT PICKS

2013: Nathan MacKinnon
2012: Nail Yakupov
2011: Ryan Nugent-Hopkins
2010: Taylor Hall
2009: John Tavares
2008: Steven Stamkos
2007: Patrick Kane
2006: Erik Johnson
2005: Sidney Crosby
2004: Alexander Ovechkin
2003: Marc-Andre Fleury
2002: Rick Nash
2001: Ilya Kovalchuk
2000: Rick DiPietro

and event. My wife, Lisa, and I talked before booking the trip and decided this is a once in a lifetime type opportunity," said Greenwood. "This was a young player who I had not only coached but taught in school, and he was now being drafted to the NHL. We knew he would be a top-three pick. So we went down and made a weekend of it in New York and New Jersey. We were sitting about ten rows back from the MacKinnons when his name was called. It was very exciting. We then got to spend some time afterwards in the Colorado suite with them, and it's something I'll never forget."

7 NHL ROOKIE SEASON

On July 9, 2013, Nathan MacKinnon signed his first professional contract, inking a three-year entry-level deal with the Colorado Avalanche. He was only the third seventeen-year-old hockey player drafted first overall in twenty-six years.

"The signing of this first NHL contract represents another step towards becoming a professional hockey player," MacKinnon said in a prepared statement released to the media by the Colorado Avalanche. "I am excited and thrilled to have been drafted by the Avalanche, and I am already working very hard in order to be ready physically and mentally for training camp."

Joe Sakic, the team's executive VP, was excited to have the rookie on board too: "We are happy to have Nathan under contract and anxious to see him at training camp," he said. "His presence will bring additional speed and talent to our team, as well as a lot of excitement to our fans."

There seemed to be little doubt that MacKinnon would make the Colorado roster in September: first overall draft choices are usually fast-tracked to the NHL and not returned to their junior teams. By signing the contract, both he and the Avalanche moved one step closer getting the teenage sensation in an NHL uniform within three months' time.

NATHAN MACKINNON'S CONTRACT

▷ NHL salary per year for three years: $925,000 (maximum allowed under league rules)

▷ Performance bonuses: $2.85 million

▷ Signing bonuses: $92,500

▷ Cap hit: $3,775,000

MacKinnon was the first player to be selected first overall by the Avalanche since the franchise moved to Denver, Colorado, in 1995. The Avalanche/Québec Nordiques franchise had drafted first overall on three previous occasions: 1989 (Mats Sundin), 1990 (Owen Nolan), and 1991 (Eric Lindros).

Following a disastrous 2012–13 regular season (the team finished 29th overall in the NHL standings), the organization was looking to MacKinnon to inject some life into the team and help it harken back to the mid-1990s and early 2000s when the Avalanche were competing for the Stanley Cup on a yearly basis. As the team's play declined, so too did attendance at the Pepsi Center in Denver. Crowds on some nights dipped as low as ten thousand in an arena that seats eighteen thousand. Bringing in a young star meant a new opportunity to attract fans; fans who would likely see MacKinnon at the top of his game since he would be playing alongside Gabriel Landeskog (the number-two overall pick in 2011) and Matt Duchene (the number-three overall pick in 2009).

MacKinnon was still two months shy of his eighteenth birthday, and instead of getting ready for university or some other form of traditional post-high-school life, he was on his way to the National Hockey League.

Nathan during a game against the Calgary Flames on December 4, 2013. THE CANADIAN PRESS / LARRY MACDOUGAL

OFF-SEASON TRAINING

During the summer following the draft and leading into his rookie season, MacKinnon trained with Sidney Crosby. Surprisingly, even though the two came from the same town and shared the same agent, they had never struck up a friendship. That changed in the summer of 2013.

Crosby took MacKinnon under his wing and took pride in the opportunities awaiting his fellow Cole Harbour native. "You're proud to see a young guy like that, coming from your hometown, do well," said Crosby.

Crosby and MacKinnon were inseparable in the weeks leading into the 2012–13 NHL regular season; they trained together and prepared for the upcoming season.

"Sid's a great guy to work out with. He's obviously a hard worker and the best player in the game," MacKinnon told CTV's Rick Grant. "To get to skate and train with him, it's a lot of fun. We do this six days a week. It's been good. I'm working with Andy O'Brien [Crosby's personal trainer] and it's been going really well. He's set it up really well with some good skates and I'm sure it will continue that way. You don't get here with magic, you put the work in. It's also fun."

The summer training experience would lay the foundation for a mutually beneficial friendship. Crosby and MacKinnon hit it off immediately and are often seen training or socializing together throughout Nova Scotia and the Maritimes.

"Having eight years' difference between Nathan and Sidney left enough time where their paths did not cross until Nathan was entering his Mooseheads experience," said Nathan's mother, Kathy. "Nathan began training under the guidance of Sidney's trainer, Andy O'Brien, which eventually led to the two of them training together on a regular basis. The summer after Nathan was drafted, he was training consistently on and off the ice and their friendship became closer."

In addition to being his training partner, Crosby also provided guidance for his younger friend. "Sidney has been a great mentor to Nathan," said Kathy MacKinnon. "Nathan is so appreciative of the fact that they can prepare for each season together

RUNNING IN THE SAND DUNES

Sidney Crosby and Nathan MacKinnon took their off-season training routine to Prince Edward Island's Brackley Beach on Canada Day weekend, just a few days after the 2013 NHL entry draft. Overseeing the rigorous training routine was Andy O'Brien, who is now regarded as one of the top strength and conditioning coaches in the industry. O'Brien told sports fitness blogger Jeff Angus, "The landscape in PEI is so beautiful, and there are many areas in which you can find great dunes and hills for training (you have to be cautious to avoid areas that are protected and not for running). There are also many different types of sand, which gives you variety from a training standpoint. While the players certainly enjoy the beauty of the environment in PEI, it is extremely intense. I've seen many athletes humbled by the sand. Sid has more than ten years of experience in that sand and is pretty dominant. We're still waiting for someone who can give him a run for his money!"

at home. They push each other and take great pride in doing so. As much as they take their training seriously, they do take time out for golf and tennis, enjoying their summer [at] home."

LIVING WITH GIGUÈRE

Housing teenaged rookies with established veterans has become a bit of a trend in the NHL over the past several years. Young players away from home for the first time, making hundreds of thousands of dollars—sometimes millions—need companionship, mentoring, and (possibly) chaperoning.

In Denver, MacKinnon was paired with Avalanche goalie Jean-Sébastien Giguère. Giguère was a perfect fit in many ways: like MacKinnon, he once starred for the Halifax Mooseheads—the team later retired his number, 47.

"I'm excited," MacKinnon said on the week he was set to move in with Giguère's family. "He played for Halifax, I played for Halifax, so we have kind of a connection there. And his wife is from Nova Scotia as well. He's won a Stanley Cup, so he's a very experienced player, and I'm looking forward to it. I've lived at home the last couple of years, so I didn't do much cooking or anything like that, so I think it's best that I live with somebody right now."

Giguère, for his part, was excited about billeting MacKinnon: "I think it's good for a young guy like that to be in a family environment," he said. "But sometimes, he will need to have some freedom as well. I'm not his dad. I'm going to give him some guidelines and I am going to share my experience with him, but at the end of the day, he's eighteen years old. He's an adult. I've never done this before, so this will be a new experience for myself and my wife and my kids. We've made it so he has some privacy in the house, a nice little setup, and hopefully it's going to click for everybody. My kids are super excited. They have a new buddy to play with."

For Nathan's parents, having their son live with the Giguères was a relief.

Shawn Horcoff (10) of the Dallas Stars tries to steal the puck from Nathan during a game on September 26, 2013.

"Jean-Sébastien was a big brother to Nate in every sense of the word," said Kathy. "We believe living with the Giguères was a huge component to why Nathan had great success his first year. JS's wife, Kristen, and their three boys, Maxime, Luka, and Felix, welcomed Nate like family, and that relationship will continue for a lifetime. Maxime and Luka actually told their teachers that both their father and their brother played for the Avalanche! For the Giguères to open up their home to a complete stranger for a busy family of five was beyond kind. We have the upmost respect for the Giguères and always will."

The NHL season was fast approaching and although MacKinnon was fairly confident he would make the Avalanche, he was training as if it were a long shot. "Anything can happen and I don't want to jinx myself," said MacKinnon. "It looks pretty good right now but I still need to earn a spot."

MACKINNON'S NHL DEBUT

To no one's surprise, Nathan MacKinnon made it onto the Colorado Avalanche's roster for the 2013–14 season. MacKinnon, who turned eighteen on September 1, 2013, became the youngest player in Avalanche franchise history to make his NHL debut. It was a moment he had been hoping for since he was seven years old, and working towards since he was thirteen, when the serious speculation that he would one day reach the NHL began. When the moment finally came, the young star was an instant success.

Kathy, Graham, and Sarah were all in the rink for Nathan's first NHL game, and MacKinnon admits he had quite a few pre-game jitters. He finished his first game as a professional hockey player with 2 assists, 15:30 in ice time, and 1 shot on goal, helping his team beat the Anaheim Ducks 6–1. His family was there, cheering with pride.

"Eighteen thousand fans excited for the season to begin, loud energy in the air, anticipation of the start of the game, hearing your son's name as they introduced the team was all so exciting," said Kathy. "We were so proud. I remember Graham and I discussing where the journey of hockey has taken Nathan, the people he has met, the work and dedication he has put into it. Watching him skate on the ice that first game, once again, was our son's dream becoming a reality right before our eyes."

MacKinnon had 4 assists in his first 5 NHL games before scoring his first career goal on October 12, 2013, versus the Washington Capitals. The milestone goal came in the second period when the Avalanche were on a power play. Paul Stastny got a backhand pass from Gabriel Landeskog, and Stastny quickly shovelled the puck to MacKinnon who was all alone in front of the net. As MacKinnon celebrated with teammates, Statsny went to the net to retrieve the puck as a souvenir for MacKinnon.

The Avalanche started the season with a remarkable 6–0 record, and MacKinnon quickly emerged as one of the team's offensive leaders with 1 goal and 6 assists. He was off to a very strong start—but the best was still to come.

On October 21, MacKinnon and the Colorado Avalanche faced Crosby and the Pittsburgh Penguins for the first time. The comparisons between the two players were difficult to ignore: eight years earlier, eighteen-year-old Sidney Crosby had scored 10 points through the first 8 games of his rookie season with the Penguins. MacKinnon already had 7 points in his first 8 games with the Avalanche. They were friends and off-season training partners but on this night, for the first time, they were opponents.

During the game, however, a Crosby-MacKinnon showdown never really happened. Neither one scored any points in a game dominated by Avalanche goalie Jean-Sébastien Giguère. Giguère stopped all 34

Sidney Crosby (87) works the puck around Nathan MacKinnon during a game in Pittsburgh on October 21, 2013.
ASSOCIATED PRESS / GENE J. PUSKAR

shots for a 1–0 Colorado victory. Crosby had a season-high 7 shots on goal and played more than 26 minutes. MacKinnon had 2 shots with only 10:54 in ice time.

On March 6, 2014, MacKinnon, as a rookie, did something most NHLers never do in an entire career: he broke a record set by Wayne Gretzky. In a game against the Detroit Red Wings, MacKinnon assisted André Benoit on an overtime goal to win 3–2. That assist extended MacKinnon's point-scoring streak to thirteen games, snapping the record for eighteen-year-old players set by Gretzky during the 1979–80 season. "It's pretty cool," MacKinnon said. "I want to be as consistent as possible. [Gretzky] probably doubled my point to-tal in those games." Although MacKinnon was leading all the NHL rookies with 22 goals and 51 points, he was far off the pace of Gretzky, who finished his rookie season with 51 goals and 137 points.

2013–14 WESTERN CONFERENCE STANDINGS

Team	Wins	Losses	Points
Anaheim	54	20	116
Colorado	52	22	112
St. Louis	52	23	111
San Jose	51	22	111
Chicago	46	21	107
Los Angeles	46	28	100
Minnesota	43	27	98
Dallas	40	31	91
Phoenix	37	30	89
Nashville	38	32	88
Winnipeg	37	35	84
Vancouver	36	35	83
Calgary	35	40	77
Edmonton	29	44	67

The Colorado bench congratulating Nathan after scoring against the Dallas Stars on January 27, 2014.

ASSOCIATED PRESS / TONY GUTIERREZ

The Avalanche had a remarkably successful season, and finished second in the Western Conference standings, third-best overall. MacKinnon had 63 regular-season points and played in all 82 games.

Joe Sakic was quick to point out that while expectations had been high for MacKinnon's rookie season, he had surpassed them all. Sakic drew a straight line, connecting MacKinnon's performance to his new head coach. "I think Patrick Roy did a good job with him, not giving him too much right away, started him without that pressure. He's really grown and learned the game," Sakic said. "What I'm most impressed of is we all knew what he could do with the puck and his speed. What he's learned away from the puck has been very impressive to me. Having Patrick and this coaching staff and some of the older veterans, he's listened and learned."

2014 NHL STANLEY CUP PLAYOFFS

The Colorado Avalanche were back in the post-season—and pride had been restored

2013–14 ROOKIE SCORING LEADERS

Player, team	Games played	Goals	Assists	Points	+/-
1. Nathan MacKinnon , Colorado	82	24	39	63	+20
2. Ondrej Palat, Tampa Bay	81	23	36	59	+32
3. Tyler Johnson, Tampa Bay	82	24	26	50	+23
4. Torey Krug, Boston	79	16	24	40	+18
5. Nick Bjugstad, Florida	76	16	22	38	-14

in a franchise known for its winning tradition since moving from Québec City for the 1995–96 season. Their first year in Denver, the Avalanche won the Stanley Cup—a remarkable accomplishment that helped the team forge a quick bond with the fans in Colorado. That bond was strengthened when the Avalanche won their second Cup in 2001. Over its first decade in Denver, the team made the playoffs ten straight times, won two Stanley Cups, and reached the Western Conference final an additional four times. Much of that winning tradition was lost between 2006 and 2013, when the Avalanche missed the playoffs five times in seven years.

MacKinnon wasn't the only reason for the Avalanche's resurgence but he was one of the biggest. Now, with his first full season behind him, he was poised to continue his torrid pace into the playoffs.

The Avalanche opened the post-season on home ice on April 17, 2014, with a 5–4 overtime victory against the Minnesota Wild. "I had some butterflies, but they went away pretty quickly," MacKinnon told ESPN after game one. "When we focus on winning, everything else goes away." When asked how he was handling his first NHL playoffs, MacKinnon responded, "It's the NHL, it's really different. This is a new experience for sure. It's obviously faster, more intense."

MacKinnon's strong play continued in game two: he scored 1 goal and added 3 assists, helping Colorado take a 4–2 win and a 2–0 series lead. MacKinnon and linemates Gabriel Landeskog and Paul Stastny were responsible for all 4 goals.

"The skills he's got, the way he skates—I haven't seen anything like it," said Landeskog, who scored twice, with both goals assisted by MacKinnon. "You realize he's eighteen," said Stastny. "He's hungry, that's what makes him a good player. He doesn't [just] rely on his skill."

MacKinnon's pace could not continue forever—and it didn't. He was pointless in games three and four as Minnesota rallied for two wins to even the series 2–2.

Nathan celebrates his game-winning goal against the Calgary Flames on December 6, 2013.
THE CANADIAN PRESS/LARRY MACDOUGAL

But MacKinnon and Colorado both rebounded in game five. MacKinnon assisted on 2 goals in regulation time, and the teams stood at a 3–3 tie after 60 minutes. The game went to sudden-death overtime: the first goal would end it. The winning goal was the result of a failed zone-clearing attempt by Minnesota that resulted in Colorado shovelling the puck into the zone at the bottom of the circle. MacKinnon retrieved it, missed on his first attempt, and then scored the overtime winner—arguably the biggest goal of his rookie year—to help his team get the win and a 3–2 series lead.

Head Coach Patrick Roy had told MacKinnon before the game that he wanted him to improve his forecheck and compete harder for the puck in the offensive zone. MacKinnon listened, and as a result was clearly improving as the game progressed.

MacKinnon's offensive output dried up after game five, as he was scoreless in the final two games of the series. Minnesota won both games, including a heartbreaking 5–4 overtime win in game seven. Colorado would not advance to the next round of the playoffs. Despite the loss, the Avalanche and MacKinnon had sent the message that they were forces to be reckoned with for years to come.

"We believe in ourselves, and it's hard to see that it's over," coach Patrick Roy said. "I'm sure tomorrow is going to hurt more thinking it's over because [right now] we still have the emotion of the game."

His rookie superstar agreed.

"It tarnishes the year a lot," said MacKinnon, who had 2 goals and 8 assists

Sweden's Niclas Andersén battles Canada's Nathan MacKinnon (29) for the puck during the 2014 IIHF World Championship in Belarus. RICHARD WOLOWICZ / HHOF-IIHF IMAGES

in the series. "We wanted to make a run here and we had a chance twice to win the series, once in game six and obviously tonight. It's tough to describe what went on. We've got to wait until September to get things going again, which is going to be a long summer, especially watching the playoffs. It's going to be tough."

Since his first NHL season was over, MacKinnon agreed to play for Team Canada at the 2014 IIHF World Hockey Championship in Minsk, Belarus. Like Sidney Crosby before him, MacKinnon joined the team at eighteen. Unfortunately, Canada did not perform well and finished the tournament in fifth place.

8
AWARDS AND ACCOLADES

On April 23, 2014, Nathan MacKinnon, Tyler Johnson, and Ondrej Palat were named the three finalists for the 2013–14 Calder Memorial Trophy for NHL Rookie of the Year. Johnson and MacKinnon had each scored 24 goals that season, and were tied for the NHL rookie scoring lead. Palat was the second leading NHL rookie scorer with 59 points.

MacKinnon was the favourite of the three to win the award, based on several statistical categories: he had finished first overall amongst the first-year players with 63 points, 24 goals (tied for first), 39 assists, 8 power play goals, and 5 game-winning goals by a rookie (also tied for first).

COMPARING NOVA SCOTIANS' FIRST FULL YEAR BY POINTS

Year	Player	Team	GP	G	A	P
2005–06	Sidney Crosby	Penguins	81	38	63	102
1978–79	Bobby Smith	North Stars	80	30	44	74
2013–14	Nathan MacKinnon	Avalanche	82	24	39	63
1981–82	Paul MacLean	Jets	74	36	25	61
1983–84	Al MacInnis	Flames	51	11	34	45
2010–11	Brad Marchand	Bruins	77	21	20	41
1984–85	Mike McPhee	Canadiens	70	17	22	39
1993–94	Glen Murray	Bruins	81	18	13	31
2000–01	Colin White	Devils	82	1	19	20
1992–93	Cam Russell	Blackhawks	67	2	4	6

The 2014 NHL Awards took place on June 24, 2014, in Las Vegas, Nevada, and MacKinnon became the youngest NHL Rookie of the Year ever. He received 130 first-place votes of the 137 ballots cast, making the decision almost unanimous.

After winning the Calder Trophy, MacKinnon was ecstatic and grateful for the opportunity he had been given. He had become the second Avalanche player in a row to win the honour. On the podium, with his trophy in hand, he thanked his family "for helping me for as long as I can remember." His remarks were brief, but when he spoke with the media afterward he reflected: "I just wanted to try to make an immediate impact and try to help the team win every night. Some nights I did, some nights I didn't, but I definitely learned a lot from the season. It's cool. I was very fortunate to be brought into a good team."

MacKinnon's childhood coach and teacher, Jon Greenwood, was proud of the rookie's accomplishments: "He never ceases to surprise me," he said. "I knew he'd make an impact right away because of his speed

Nathan poses with the Calder Trophy after winning the award for top rookie in the NHL on June 24, 2014.
ASSOCIATED PRESS / JOHN LOCHER

and competitiveness but wasn't sure to what degree. There were a lot of nights I thought he was one of the best players on

NATHAN MACKINNON'S AWARDS

Calder Memorial Trophy (NHL's top rookie)	2013–2014
NHL All-Rookie Team	2013–2014
QMJHL Ed Chynoweth Trophy (Memorial Cup leading scorer)	2012–2013
QMJHL Stafford Smythe Memorial Trophy (Memorial Cup MVP)	2012–2013
QMJHL Memorial Cup All-star Team	2012–2013
QMJHL Second All-star Team	2012- 2013

Nathan scores on Winnipeg Jets goalie Ondrej Pavelec during a shootout on December 11, 2014.

ASSOCIATED PRESS / DAVID ZALUBOWSKI

Darren Cossar, executive director, Hockey Nova Scotia:

Nathan MacKinnon has been great for hockey in Nova Scotia; he followed in the very big footsteps of Sidney and did so under a microscope right here in his hometown. To have Nathan follow Sidney was the perfect storm for the development of hockey in our province. It showed all the positives of the game, that our development system is working, and kids from Nova Scotia have every opportunity to move on within the game, and that hard work and dedication can pay off.

the ice, which is truly remarkable for an eighteen-year-old rookie in the best league in the world."

Those who were now seeing MacKinnon play for the first time were also impressed. "Nathan is one of the top potential quick-strike offensive players in the NHL today," said *NHL on NBC* analyst Pierre McGuire. "His speed and release on his shots helps to make him a lethal scoring threat every time he is on the ice. Much like other great scoring stars in NHL history, Nathan has the ability to lift you out of your seat every time he touches the puck."

The Halifax *Chronicle-Herald*'s editorial section on June 25, 2014:

> *Congratulations to Crosby and MacKinnon for winning top NHL awards—and take a bow, hockey lovers, supporters, and coaches of Cole Harbour, for demonstrating that when a Nova Scotia community puts its heart and mind into nurturing great hockey players, it can produce two of the best in the world.*

That same year, Patrick Roy, also in his rookie year behind a NHL bench, was named the Jack Adams Trophy winner as the NHL's coach of the year. Roy helped turn the franchise around, coaching Colorado to a third-place finish in the overall league standings after the team finished 29th the previous season.

9
YEAR TWO WITH THE AVALANCHE

In Nathan MacKinnon's first year with the Colorado Avalanche, the team soared with 112 points. MacKinnon's 63 points and Calder Trophy win set high expectations for the following year.

In the off-season MacKinnon brought his training regimen to a new level. He was still working with trainer Andy O'Brien and he put on twelve to thirteen pounds of muscle and maintained 6 percent body fat. He came to the Avalanche's 2014–15 September training camp prepared and in the best shape of his life.

"I don't think I was playing with much confidence [last season]," MacKinnon told Yahoo! Sports. "I was scared to make plays, scared to mess up. The switch kind of flipped after Christmas. I just figured I need to start playing my game. I don't think it was as good a season as everybody's saying it was. Obviously I had to learn some stuff. There were a few bumps in the road. I expect more out of me. I feel like I can really take the next step this season. I had a year of growth, but now I need to prove that I can be a dominant player in the league more than last year."

Although the pre-season held so much promise, the Avalanche sat with a mediocre record of 2–4–4 after ten games. In his first two games, MacKinnon had yet to register a point. Through seven games, he had only 3 assists and had yet to score a goal. Through ten games, MacKinnon had just 4 assists and still no goals. Nathan MacKinnon was in danger of suffering the dreaded "sophomore slump" that many players before him had endured.

"I think [the sophomore slump] is a bunch of crap," Avalanche centre Matt Duchene told the *Denver Post*. Duchene experienced a similar slump at the beginning of his second season with Colorado. "If [MacKinnon] just keeps skating and working hard, he's going to get one fluky goal and it's going to take off from there."

For MacKinnon's head coach Patrick Roy, a slow start to a season or even a long-term slump was no reason for panic. The Avalanche were still a young team, but a team on the rise. They were developing, and any growing pains they endured were all part of a process that would lead to sustained success. "It will happen for him," said Roy.

"It doesn't have to be the perfect goal. Just put pucks on net and good things happen."

The bounce MacKinnon was waiting for finally came on October 30, 2014, when the Avalanche beat the New York Islanders 5–0 and MacKinnon scored his first 2 goals of the season. "I figured a goal would come sooner or later," said MacKinnon. "Obviously, a little later than I wanted, but it's all in the past now."

LIVING WITH MAXIME TALBOT

Jean-Sébastien Giguère retired after the 2013–14 season, so in his second year, MacKinnon moved in with Maxime Talbot.

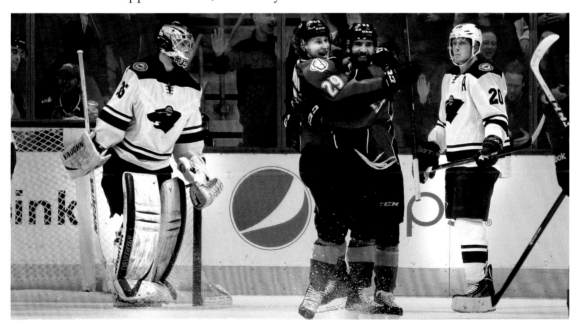

Nathan (29) celebrates with Maxime Talbot (25) after scoring on Minnesota Wild goalie Darcy Kuemper on January 30, 2014. ASSOCIATED PRESS / BARRY GUTIERREZ

Talbot and MacKinnon had a personal connection through their mutual friendship with Sidney Crosby, who was a former Penguins linemate of Talbot's.

"I felt like I knew Nate before I met him because of Sid, and talking to Sid," said Talbot in an interview with the *Denver Post*. "And I think Nate felt the same way because he cheered the Penguins for so long. You know, the Penguins are his team. When we won the Cup and brought the Cup to Nova Scotia, I went with Sid, and Nate was age thirteen on the side of the road, waving at us. That's pretty crazy to think about it. And when I was younger I always respected players who took the young guys in, guys like Mario Lemieux taking in Sid [in Pittsburgh], Danny Brière with young Claude Giroux [in Philadelphia]. Now, with a number of years under my belt, I'm proud to be doing it."

MacKinnon and Talbot gelled well: "I know how to act. I'm respectful to their house, their children, clean up for myself. I'm still a teenager, so I make some mistakes around the house, but overall things have been going pretty well," MacKinnon said.

But the domestic harmony of the second season was disrupted in early March when Talbot was traded to the Boston Bruins, and MacKinnon lost his roommate. Just three days later, the Avalanche announced that MacKinnon was injured and would miss the rest of the regular season with a fractured foot.

The injury occurred on February 22 in a game against the Tampa Bay Lightning. At first, the team thought MacKinnon would be able to play the rest of the season, but after playing five days later against Dallas, his pain was too severe and a fracture was finally diagnosed. MacKinnon was sidelined for six to eight weeks, which meant his season was over.

It was a big setback for Colorado, a team suffering through a dismal season that

Nathan with a fractured foot (L) and Avalanche defenceman Tyson Barrie courtside at an NBA game in Denver on March 27, 2015. ASSOCIATED PRESS / DAVID ZALUBOWSK

Team Canada locker room (L-R): Sidney Crosby, Nathan MacKinnon, and Matt Duchene celebrate their gold medal win over Russia at the 2015 IIHF World Championship. ANDRE RINGUETTE / HHOF-IIHF IMAGES

featured injuries to key players all year long. "It's never good news when you're losing a player like Nate, especially in a key moment in our season," said head coach Patrick Roy. "It's been a year like this and we're going to have to win games without him."

MacKinnon could have returned to the ice if the Avalanche had made the playoffs, but the team finished 7 points out of a playoff spot, in eleventh place in the Western Conference. Ultimately, MacKinnon's second season statistics were disappointing: he finished with just 14 goals and 38 points over 64 games.

2015 IIHF WORLD HOCKEY CHAMPIONSHIP

By May, when the 2015 IIHF World Hockey Championship in the Czech Republic rolled around, MacKinnon was healthy enough to compete for Team Canada. Joined by fellow Cole Harbour native Sidney Crosby, MacKinnon helped lead the team to total domination at the tournament. Canada went undefeated through ten games and won the gold medal, the country's first World Championship win since 2007. In 10 games, MacKinnon scored 4 goals and added 5 assists.

Looking back on MacKinnon's second season as a professional, Mooseheads General Manager Cam Russell felt no concerns about the drop in productivity. In fact, Russell fully expects MacKinnon to rise and meet the expectations placed on him prior to being drafted in 2013. "He's too much of competitor not to get better," said Russell. "He has so much heart. The Crosbys and the MacKinnons of the world have world-class skill and drive. He's got this drive to be the best."

MacKinnon heads into his third season looking to bounce back from a sophomore slide with adversity and injury. Year two is behind him, and by all accounts he has trained harder in the off-season than ever before. He is bigger, stronger, and faster than he has ever been. Nathan MacKinnon is well positioned to fulfil his potential while cementing his status as one of the game's young rising stars.

APPENDIX
NATHAN MACKINNON
CAREER STATS

Nathan MacKinnon suited up for Team Canada during the 2015 IIHF World Championship.
ANDRE RINGUETTE / HHOF-IIHF IMAGES

INTERNATIONAL

Year	Team	Division	GP	G	A	PTS
2010–11	Canada Atlantic	U-17	5	5	3	8
201–12	Canada Atlantic	U-17	5	1	3	4
2012–13	Canada	U-18	5	5	6	11
2012–13	Canada	U-20	6	0	1	1
2013–14	Canada	WC	8	1	3	4
2014–15	Canada	WC	10	4	5	9
Totals			39	16	21	37

JUNIOR AND PROFESSIONAL

Year	Team	Division	GP	G	A	PTS
2011–2012	Halifax Mooseheads	QMJHL	58	31	47	78
2012–2013	Halifax Mooseheads	QMJHL	44	32	43	75
2013–2014	Colorado Avalanche	NHL	82	24	39	63
2014–2015	Colorado Avalanche	NHL	64	14	24	38

MACKINNON TIMELINE

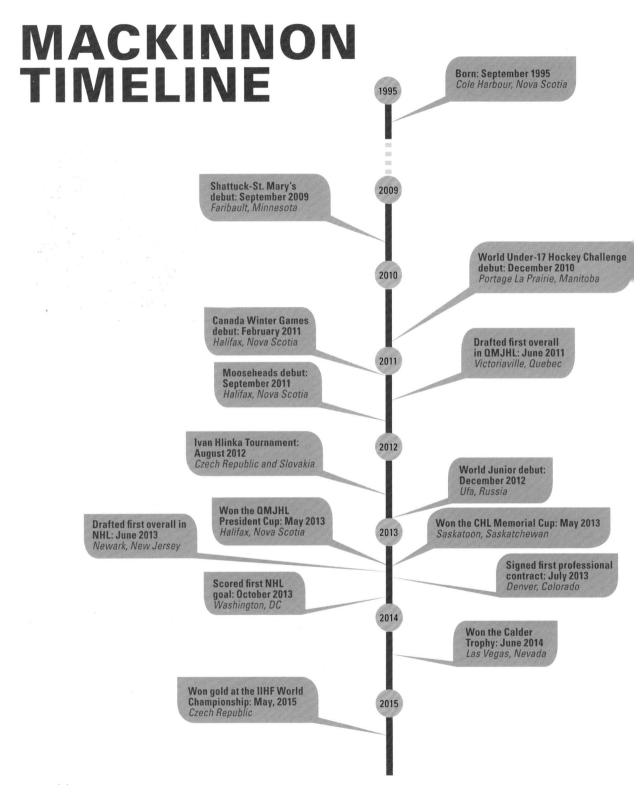

1995

Born: September 1995
Cole Harbour, Nova Scotia

2009

Shattuck-St. Mary's debut: September 2009
Faribault, Minnesota

2010

World Under-17 Hockey Challenge debut: December 2010
Portage La Prairie, Manitoba

2011

Canada Winter Games debut: February 2011
Halifax, Nova Scotia

Drafted first overall in QMJHL: June 2011
Victoriaville, Quebec

Mooseheads debut: September 2011
Halifax, Nova Scotia

2012

Ivan Hlinka Tournament: August 2012
Czech Republic and Slovakia

World Junior debut: December 2012
Ufa, Russia

2013

Won the QMJHL President Cup: May 2013
Halifax, Nova Scotia

Won the CHL Memorial Cup: May 2013
Saskatoon, Saskatchewan

Drafted first overall in NHL: June 2013
Newark, New Jersey

Signed first professional contract: July 2013
Denver, Colorado

Scored first NHL goal: October 2013
Washington, DC

2014

Won the Calder Trophy: June 2014
Las Vegas, Nevada

Won gold at the IIHF World Championship: May, 2015
Czech Republic

2015